Jen
Cokesbury Bk Store
Richmond Va.
17 April 1968

Receiving God's Fullness

WALLACE D. CHAPPELL

Receiving God's Fullness

"From his fullness have we all received."
—JOHN 1:16 (R.S.V.)

Abingdon Press—NEW YORK • NASHVILLE

RECEIVING GOD'S FULLNESS

Copyright © 1960 by Abingdon Press

Library of Congress Catalog Card Number: 60-9196

SET UP, PRINTED, AND BOUND BY THE
PARTHENON PRESS, AT NASHVILLE,
TENNESSEE, UNITED STATES OF AMERICA

To those **loyal friends** along the Nolichucky River
whose lives inspired their young
preacher and still point the way
in the quest for God's fullness.

Introduction

Wallace Chappell is a younger preacher. He loves to preach. He has preaching blood in his veins, coming from a family of preachers who have made notable Kingdom contributions across the years. He believes profoundly in the power of the gospel, and feels deeply the sense of its wonder and its glory. He demonstrates constantly the possibilities of warm-hearted, imaginative preaching, as he is called for special evangelistic services, but particularly as he carries on his regular ministry in a city church which is ministering effectively in a changing community.

These sermons speak for themselves. They have about them a strong hortatory note often lacking in many sermons. There is in them a warmth and sense of urgency which make for a strong persuasive appeal. Best of all they gladly lift up him who promised to draw all men unto himself.

Roy H. Short

Contents

CHAPTER TWO

His Coming

His Coming

"I have come that they may have life and have it to the full."
—John 10:10 (Moffatt)

• "I have come" is the heart of the gospel. The entrance of Christ into our world is God's good news. A Christian in pre-Communist Russia was arrested for refusing to serve in the army and was brought to trial. After listening to his testimony, the judge remarked, "You are acting as if the kingdom of God had already come." The courageous disciple answered, "It has come for me."

To be sure there are multitudes of the earth's people who have not heard the name Jesus. There are great throngs, too, who are familiar with his name but do not practice his principles. So long as this is the case, we cannot assert dogmatically that the kingdom of God has come. And yet in the personal realm when one has a fearless faith in the King, as did this Christian in the Russian courtroom, then the kingdom has come. God assuredly reigns in our world when his presence rules in our lives.

He has come. But his coming to earth means nothing unless with open heart we pray, "Come to me, abide with me, my Lord Emmanuel."

Now what was the purpose of his coming? Why does he always seek entrance into our world, into our lives?

I

Jesus came to reveal the character of God; he came to show us what God is like.

Samuel taught about a God to whom obedience was the first concern. Amos proclaimed a God of justice. Hosea preached a God of mercy. Hope was the theme of Isaiah's ministry, and Micah felt that this God of hope would eventually reign throughout the world. But Jesus came saying that God's essential character is love.

The world into which Jesus was born hungered for this love, this good news. The Roman Empire was in constant war. Slavery had long been part of the Hebrew culture. Paganism with its zeal for idolatry was as far from God as both war and slavery. Jewish communities were divided by discord and split by strife. Christ's message to the warring world was peace. His tidings to slaveholder and slave were good will toward men. The gospel he declared to pagan and Jew was that the kingdom of love is present and he as its king had come to invest all who were willing with its royalty.

This love was proclaimed in parable. He told a story about a loving father who went out to meet his wayward

12

son, forgave the boy's past actions, and welcomed him again into the communion of the home. He spoke of a shepherd who was so concerned about one lost lamb that he could not rest until he found it. And he told of the Samaritan who would not pass by one severely beaten but went to him, bound up his wounds, and took him to a lodging place.

This love was proved in practice. The lame healed, the leper cleansed, the sick cured, the fallen lifted—all these could testify that Christ's love had been at work. And on the cross, denied and betrayed and dying, his only thought for those who were killing him was intercession for their forgiveness.

The good news he offered then, he offers now. And the need is equally desperate as when he first opened the gates to the new realm and bade entrance. Peace is far from being realized in our world. Social tolerance is the dream of every Christian but far from reality. Love still reaches with nail-scarred hands to embrace the objects of divine affection. But our world, our culture, even our Church often seem a long distance from Christ because we as individuals continually refuse the Godlikeness he seeks to bestow.

When we fail to receive the love he longs to give, we are then incapable of sharing his transforming gospel. Yet this is our supreme purpose in life. If Christ came to reveal God, then we are born to reveal Christ. Just as certainly as he commanded his early followers to bear fruit, so he commissions us to do the same. Our only hope for

13

such an endeavor lies in our willingness to allow the world to see Jesus in us. If there were more of us revealing him, there would be more seeking him.

When Peter and John were being examined by the council, they preached with such a holy boldness that even the elders and scribes recognized that they had been with Jesus. Remember, people can tell. If you remind that lost man of Jesus, how much greater your chance of winning him. If those with whom you work can see something Godlike in your life, they may be eternally changed, for such religion influences all whom it touches. If that mother and father across the street can see kinship with the Master in your family life, it is more than just a possibility that they will desire a home with such joy. Your witness is on trial each day, not before a council but before the world.

Not long ago I sat in the office of an outstanding Christian teacher. While waiting for him to come in I happened to glance at a book in his library. It was a treatise dealing with five of the world's great philosophies: Stoicism, Epicurianism, Aristotelianism, Platonism, and Christianity. Someone had presented the book to him as a gift and had written on the flyleaf, "To the man who makes me believe in the greatest of the philosophies—Christianity." But Christianity is more than just a philosophy; it is a way of life and it was the life of the professor that had brought such conviction to his friend.

By the way we live, are we causing people to believe in

14

Christ? Our supreme obligation and privilege is reflecting the Redeemer.

II

Jesus came to remove the power of sin.

The first thing we must note is that Jesus incessantly seeks sin. He said that the Son of man came to seek the lost. Christ is continually searching for hearts to respond to his will. If we have never yielded to the Master's personal invitation, we may be sure that kindly, lovingly, constantly Jesus is looking for us. And the fact that we are restless and dissatisfied, even when we make great material gains, indicates that our soul nourishes a divine discontent. Christ is on a man hunt, and each of us is that man! No matter how far from him at times we may be, in the depths of our heart we know we are haunted by good. And the good ever convicts because Jesus ever calls. He wants to take from us every weakness. He wants to give us strength of spirit where now there is cowardice of character.

I used to think that verse in the Old Testament, "Be sure your sin will find you out," meant that Jesus was a kind of FBI agent and that he would catch up with my wickedness some day. Moffatt says its true meaning is "punishment for your sin will fall on you," and sin is anything that hinders total allegiance. That sin you think you control, if it is not given up, will control you. And sin's control leads inevitably to sin's wreck and ruin. I can think of no worse punishment than that. The social drink you take today might tomorrow lead to bars and poor health and lost jobs and a divorce court. That small bet you make today could tomorrow lead to laxness in responsibility and borrowed money and pawn tickets and suicide. Skipping church now and then, twice a month, and finally regularly may lead eventually to complete spiritual disintegration.

Jesus sought always to purify by placing his finger on the source of the problem. The woman of Sychar wanted to continue the discussion about water. Jesus said, "Go call your husband." Nicodemus wanted to discuss miracles. Jesus said, "You must be born anew." Peter wanted to talk about his courage in the face of danger. Jesus said, "The cock will not crow this day until you deny that you know me." He knew their supreme needs. He got at the foundations of their failures.

You have sin in your life. You are not happy, because happiness depends not on what you have but what you are. Happiness comes only when Christ is allowed entrance. But Jesus cannot enter a house that is already full. That is why he must remove before he can reside. And so he seeks out the evil things within you and at the same time shows you how little they matter in comparison to his residence in your life.

But he does more than seek the sin. He saves the sinner. He said that the Son of man came to save the lost. The chief priests, scribes, and elders, intending derision, actually spoke the truth of the gospel when they said that he saved

16

others, but could not save himself. Of course he could not. He was giving himself to save them and us.

Drinking brought a cultured man literally into the gutter. One night he made his way to a rescue mission and was soundly converted. The next day he boarded a train to go back to his wife and family. The conductor stared at him in surprise for the poverty of his clothing did not harmonize with the radiance on his face. "You look as if someone had died and left you a fortune," said the conductor.

"You are right there," the man answered; "the Lord Jesus Christ died and has given me his riches in glory."

And so he has. His hands were pierced for you. His body was broken for you. His blood was shed for you. When you allow him to find you, God's riches become yours, and the greatest wealth he gives is his ever-available presence.

III

Jesus came to rebuild the unity of believers, or to say it in another way, he came to release a togetherness of spirit and dedication.

There was religion in the world before Christ came. But it had degenerated into a form without force. It had a kind of outside piety without inside power, for its chief interest was cleansing the outside of the cup. Synagogue services of worship were held, but for the most part they were gatherings where ritual and legality substituted for regeneration and life. Now Jesus did not come to destroy the religious views or abolish the manner of worship or expel the synagogue rulers. He came to bring a freshness and a fullness to worship which all too often was monotonous and meaningless. Release, recovery, liberty—these were his rally calls to action. He came so that the great body of God's children could begin anew, could be rebuilt, restored with an unflagging buoyancy of spirit.

How did he propose to do this? How can his spirit unite us now?

First, Jesus taught personal contact with God. He declared that life which overflowed was more than merely keeping an external law. Life abundant and triumphant came because of an abiding kinship with God. He said that life eternal lay in knowing the Father.

A man had a problem and went to see Phillips Brooks about it. They talked a while and prayed together. When the man left he had a new joy on his face and a new confidence in his heart. Suddenly he remembered that he had not even mentioned to Brooks the particular issue which had been on his mind. What he needed was not an answer to his problem but contact with a victorious personality.

You meet difficulties each day. You need not meet them alone. Prepare for the hard road of life by walking the high road of love. You can face life with courage when you face it with God.

Next, Jesus taught a personal concern for others. Never did Christ come upon one in need who did not receive his full attention. This was especially true with regard to those who were looked down upon by others. Israel's "lost sheep,"

18

according to the Pharisees, were cut off from God's promises. But it was to these outcasts that Jesus made his greatest appeal. When his disciples were asked why their teacher ate with tax collectors and sinners, he answered before they had a chance that he came not to call the righteous but the sinners.

There was Matthew. He was hated because he was a Jew on the Roman payroll. One day in Capernaum as he sat at the tax office he met the Savior. His profitable business at once was forgotten, for he had seen with one look at Jesus the difference between luxury and life. The very next glimpse we have of him is at a great dinner given in honor of his Lord where other such despised collectors have been invited. From collecting taxes he had accepted his new responsibility of calling men.

The woman whom Jesus met at the well has been mentioned. There is no telling the ridicule she suffered at the hands of the respectable citizens of her town. Her life most likely had been nearly all shadow and shame. But when she meets the Master she is transformed into a city-wide evangelist.

Christ expects us to maintain that same concern, that genuine compassion for any in need of his love. Halford Luccock has said, "The church in its greatest hours has never been respectable. It has consorted with sinners. It has reached out its hands to the rag, tag, and bobtail of humanity." If we are to do Christ's bidding, this task must not be altered now.

19

I am going to pretend that I am a preacher in the city of Rome. I understand that the apostle Paul is in prison and has just received the death sentence. I secure permission to visit him in the dungeon thinking perhaps I can be of some consolation and help during his final hour. How often he had strengthened the persecuted of the young Church. But as I enter the narrow jail room, I find one who has little need for pity. Just his presence makes the prison more like a cathedral than a cell. The glow and the glory of the Damascus road encounter have not faded from his face. Suddenly I hear a door open, then the guards appear, and I know the executioner awaits his victim.

"Paul," I whisper, "do you have some word that I can take back to the people of the Church?"

"Tell them to preach the word of God," he cries triumphantly. "Tell them to be urgent in telling the good news, for I have found it to be man's only hope. And tell them that best of all, God will supply all their needs from his glorious resources in Christ Jesus."

The world is waiting. Our God is able. We must not fail.

CHAPTER TWO

His Call

"Then Jesus told his disciples, 'If any man would come after me, let him deny himself and take up his cross and follow me.'" —Matt. 16:24 (R.S.V.)

• Even the severest critics of Jesus never accused him of beating around the bush. He always spoke frankly though tenderly. But never was he more explicit than here at Caesarea when he presented the marching orders of the kingdom. "Deny yourself—take up your cross—follow me."

Earlier Jesus had spoken of the unswerving path his Messiahship must take. The multitudes, even those closest to him, were anticipating no such deliverer. As he spoke of repudiation, suffering, finally death, the crowd must have stared at him in paralyzed amazement and utter unbelief. From the startled throng Peter was the first to speak. "God forbid, Lord! This shall never happen to you," he exclaimed, thus voicing the view of the majority. For their expectation was of a king who would bring liberation, not a martyr who would suffer rejection.

21

Jesus quickly replied, "Get behind me, Satan!" meaning simply that anything less than Calvary would be futile, false, even devilish.

Then he gave the directions to discipleship, like unto the course he had chartered for himself: "If any man would come after me, let him deny himself and take up his cross and follow me." This was his announcement of action. This was his summons to service. This is his personal call to each of us today.

I

"Deny yourself." Self-denial means to "make yourself a stranger to yourself." It indicates that your own wishes should mean nothing to you if they contradict the Father's will. It affirms simply for the Christian that any way but God's way is wrong. Jesus knew this. He was able to overcome the tempter because during days and nights in the wilderness he found strength through surrender to God. When the crowds, impressed by his miracles, sought to make him King, he went into the hills. Here he found guidance for the future through the power of submission to the Father. Even at the end there was no lack of courage at Calvary because of the bravery of obedience in Gethsemane.

Self-denial or self-yielding to God is no mere sideline. It is indispensable to Christian living and vital to every spiritual experience. Hear the Master speak: "Whoever would save his life will lose it, and whoever loses his life for my sake will find it."

22

Unsurrendered self, or selfishness, blinds us to that which is essential. Self-gratification says, "I want what I want"; Self-denial says, "I want what I need." The selfish man wants his pocketbook full; the surrendered man desires treasures that neither moth nor rust consumes.

Selfishness says, "Me, my, mine"; Selflessness says, "You, yours, theirs." The results may deceive us, for the fruits of want and wealth and possession and seizure are nearly always evident and tangible. On the other hand, the rewards of the consecrated self are often intangible and unseen. There was the rich farmer. So interested was he in his barns and grain and goods that the thing of foremost importance was forgotten. Consider the rich young man. His eyes were so fixed on what he had that he rejected that supreme "one thing."

There was a college boy whose room was filled with vulgar pictures. One day his mother sent him a picture of Christ. After taking the other pictures down from the wall, he said simply, "I could not allow those cheap things to stay up there beside that face." Of course something took place in his heart before the difference was seen on the wall. If we allow self to make our choices that which matters most is neglected.

If selfishness blinds us to what is vital for our own lives, then it also blinds us to the needs of others. The Pharisee in the temple was so busy parading his own self-importance that he had no time to pray for mercy upon the publican. A man who is doing all for self never sees the poverty of another. So intent was Dives upon the material that we are not sure he even knew Lazarus lay in need at his gate.

After the first Great War, the Treaty of Versailles was drawn up in the hall of mirrors. Rita Snowden says that this fact makes it a parable. Each nation was looking to its own wishes rather than the needs of others. This was the besetting sin of James and John. Each wanted a choice place to sit in the kingdom instead of a chief place to serve in the vineyard.

The only answer to selfishness is complete giving to God.

> Let "Self" be crucified and slain
> And buried deep: and all in vain
> May efforts be to rise again,
> Unless to live for Others.[1]

II

"Take up your cross." This command given by our Lord is often misunderstood. Dr. Weatherhead says that people talk about bearing their cross when they mean getting on with their mother-in-law or bearing a twinge of rheumatism.[2] But "take up your cross" is a call to Christlikeness. It is an invitation to complete dedication involving the rejection of ease and accepting the certainty of sacrifice.

Too many of us seek a religion that is easy. Possibly the desire for ease led to the eventual downfall of Judas. He,

[1] C. D. Meigs. Used by permission.
[2] From The Transforming Friendship.

as the other disciples, thought it much easier to bring in a kingdom without bearing a cross. And when he found that Christ's way was not one of force through power but pardon through pain, it seemed too hard and looked as if it would take too long. Many people today share that same conception, but the kingdom only comes when the cross is carried.

It would have been much easier for Jesus, when he left Judea for Galilee, to go by way of Perea. That was the easy way. Going through Samaria exposed him to enemy attack due to bitter feeling between Jew and Samaritan. But there was a Gospel to be proclaimed and a town to be reached and a woman to be won. It was the way of difficulty but it was the way of discipleship.

> Must I be carried to the skies
>   On flowery beds of ease,
> While others fought to win the prize,
>   And sailed through bloody seas?
>
> Sure I must fight, if I would reign:
>   Increase my courage, Lord;
> I'll bear the toil, endure the pain,
>   Supported by Thy word.

What is the toil and pain? It is the emergence of a supreme concern, a great anxiety that manifests itself in any loving task for the sake of one in need. But the labor is never forced. The Calvary way is never a penalty imposed. It is unselfish love volunteered. To take up the cross means that you are willing to do anything for Christ which will help another.

When Parkes Cadman, the beloved minister of a generation ago, lay dying, expressions of love, prayer and pity came from both sides of the ocean. Many were from the world's prominent. None, however, was more touching than a note sent by a laboring man to the minister's home. It read, "I have no money but if Dr. Cadman needs blood, he can have all of mine."

That is the sacrifice Jesus made. He expects no less of his disciples.

III

"Follow me!"

This is Jesus' invitation to a life of service. He will lead. He will go before. It is ours to follow in faith and trust. Where does Jesus' leadership take us?

First, we are led into a life of usefulness. As a Christian cannot be evil, so a Christian cannot be neutral. We are told by the Master that we are the salt of the earth, and salt is positive. The man with the one talent did not gamble it away. He did not spend it in riotous living. He just buried it. The priest and Levite did not kick the man in the ditch who was already in serious condition. They did not laugh or make fun of his sad plight. They just passed him by. The rich man did not abuse Lazarus. He did not have him flogged for loitering. He just did nothing.

On the other hand, consider those who are doers of the

word. Once I stood where tradition tells us Mary and Martha lived. Here the Master would come when he was weary and in need of rest. They furnished him with more than a bed and meal. They gave him the strength of friendship. We remember them because they were useful.

We know very little about the lad who gave his loaves and fish. He never left his name that we might exalt. He never left his autograph that we might applaud. But he was useful when the Lord needed him and so long as kindness lives we will honor him.

Onesimus was probably a thief. We know that he was a slave and that is enough to have hidden him in the dark shadows of oblivion. But somehow he met Paul, and more important he met Paul's Christ and became useful. Onesimus is a synonym for service.

Margaret Slattery once told about a crippled newspaper boy upon whom a prominent physician took pity. He operated on the lad's legs and the surgery was successful. "Now," she said, "I would like to tell you that this newspaper boy himself became a doctor with a compassion for others in need. But I cannot do that for he was electrocuted in one of our prisons just recently."

Then, looking into the listeners' hearts as well as their eyes, she added, "Medical science could show that boy how to walk, but only God's man could show him where to walk." It is our everlasting obligation to be useful in pointing others to the way.

The second point you have already anticipated. A life of usefulness leads to a life of joyfulness.

True gladness is the outcome of true service. The psalmist wrote that the happy people are the ones who follow the Lord's teachings and give him undivided hearts. Jesus did not say blessed are the peace thinkers but the peace makers. Real happiness comes

> In being not seeming,
> In doing each day that goes by
> Some little good, not in dreaming
> Of great things to do by and by.[3]

There is a legend about a valley of roses so vast that the fragrance of the flowers perfumes the air for many miles. When one walks through the valley and reaches the end of his journey the scent is all about him and those who meet him know where he has been.[4]

As the roses leave their fragrance, communion with Christ leaves its radiance. Others will seek out the reason for such joyfulness because it is gloriously contagious.

Just before he died, Charles H. Spurgeon, the great English preacher, said to his wife, "I've had such a wonderful time with Jesus." This companionship is a joy that never ends. It is eternally ours if we follow him.

---

[3] "Nobility" by Alice Carey.
[4] Leslie Weatherhead, *Jesus and Ourselves*.

CHAPTER THREE

Wanting God

"But if from thence thou shalt seek the Lord thy God, thou shalt find him, if thou seek him with all thy heart and with all thy soul."—Deut. 4:29

• Before you can respond to the Lord's coming and answer his call you must want Christ with all your heart. Some people want to be Christian but the urge is half-hearted and the desire is not great.

Recently, during a week of evangelistic services, a man came to hear me preach each night. He was not happy with his religion and confessed to me he had not fully surrendered to the Master. We became rather intimate friends, and one night I told him that I believed his difficulty was that he did not *want* to belong completely to Jesus. "When you want to be a Christian with your entire heart, holding back nothing," I said, "you will find the true joy of salvation." It was just a few hours later that he allowed the Divine Presence to come into his life and he gave this testimony: "I prayed to want Christ."

29

Jesus said, "Blessed are those that hunger and thirst after righteousness." Do you have an actual craving for the presence of the Redeemer? Do you, with no reservations, want the Man of Galilee to possess you and use you as he wills?

I

There are several reasons why we do not completely and wholeheartedly want God. I think they are most surely true for our day.

First, we doubt the personal redemptive touch of the Master. Even within the church many do not have faith that his companionship can be intimate or his presence be actual. "The trouble is not that we think God untrue," says Harry Emerson Fosdick, "but unreal. It is one thing to believe in God; it is another thing to confront Him." [1] For some their religion is mostly hearsay and little contact. How we need to approach the Savior with childlike hearts, eager to learn, desiring to follow, ready for action.

Mental assent can never substitute for spiritual acceptance. Luke tells us that Felix had a rather accurate knowledge of the way. Yet it was a knowledge of rather than a sharing in. It was not real, not personal to him.

Jesus informed the Pharisees that they could see clouds rising in the west and know rain was on the way; that they could see the south wind blowing and be assured of scorching heat. He said, "You know how to interpret the appear-

[1] From *What Is Vital in Religion*.

30

ance of earth and sky, but why do you not know how to interpret the present time?" The answer is of course because they were not willing to give themselves sacrificially and completely to him who is the present time, the blessed Alpha and Omega.

When we draw near to the Lord humbly and with a deep yearning to know more of his love, it is amazing how warm and personal is the experience. We must enter the sacred gates of prayer not as scoffers seeking proof but sinners seeking pardon. When we do, we will come to know him just as certainly as did those with whom he walked the Galilean hills.

Then, not only do we doubt that personal relationship but so often we feel we do not need divine help. Tears and heartaches may come before we ever recognize our dependence on God. Though we may say skeptically that we do not want anyone suffering for us or bearing our sins, we need face facts no more than a moment to see we are daily spared by the price others pay. There are 25,000 graves in Korea where men died for us. A doctor takes his life in his hands in an effort to save us as he exposes himself to tuberculosis and strives to cure. Even our neighborhood policemen daily risk their lives in order that we may live safely and happily. If we need a savior, we need the Savior.

Samson reached the conclusion that he lacked nothing. A lion or an army could do little against his muscles. So he relinquished his grasp on God. But "the Philistines are upon you, Samson," and in prison, betrayed, blind and bound, he recognized that his real power had not been in his brawn but in his faith.

You may have spent most of your life in the sunshine, but the shadows are sure to come. Until now perhaps you have easily overcome obstacles, but in your own strength future hinderances might not be mastered. There are times when resolution and self-assertion will not see you through. Christ only will be adequate. And since one never knows when the shadows may fall or the snares will entangle, the truth is you need God all the time.

> I need Thee every hour;
>   Stay Thou near by;
> Temptations lose their power
>   When Thou art nigh.

> I need Thee every hour;
>   In joy or pain;
> Come quickly and abide,
>   Or life is vain.

To me, Saul is the most tragic figure in the Old Testament. If you want the story of how one can gradually collapse because of a rotting inner self, read again the first book of Samuel. When a man turns from obeying the will of God to following the dictates of his own desires and the voices of the world, fear immediately starts its disintegrating action on his soul, for fear is the opposite of trust. We read of how Saul grabbed the spoils of the Amalekites and we know that

32

he was afraid of losing his popularity with the people. We read of his raging anger toward Israel's sweet singer and we know he was afraid of forfeiting his position to David. We read of how the words, "Saul has slain his thousands and David his ten thousands," stung his pride and we know he was afraid of losing his reputation with the cheering mobs of the city. Thus failing to realize his permanent need for God, Saul who began with such promise, ended his life not as an inspiration but an utter disappointment. When you place self on the throne, moral decay has done its work.

However, the greatest reason why God is not worshiped and Christ is not followed is that we do not have the courage Jesus requires to go all out for his cause. One came to the Master in the long ago saying that he would follow Jesus wherever he went. The Lord answered that foxes had holes and birds had nests but sometimes he had nowhere to sleep at night. And we have no indication that the man made any other effort to become a disciple. If a man does not have the desire to be an out and out follower, sleeping on the ground will prove too reckless an adventure.

"There is only one religious difficulty," James Denney used to say, "—the difficulty of being religious."

I once asked Homer Rodeheaver the secret of Billy Sunday's great evangelical success. Mr. Rodeheaver had traveled with the evangelist for many years and probably knew him better than any other man. After mentioning his prayer habits and daily Bible study, he said, "Billy had a tremendous amount of courage and he hated sin." There were some Sunday techniques and characteristics we would hesitate to acquire; and yet, when we remember the great effect his ministry had upon the liquor traffic, such courage should be desired by all of Christ's followers.

Some years ago I stood in the Colosseum at Rome. As I thought of the sacrifices that had been made there, I questioned my courage as a disciple of Christ. I closed my eyes on the world about me and imagined I was standing in that same spot nineteen centuries ago. I saw the Christians appear in the arena after being driven like cattle from their dungeon cells. Then I saw the lions come upon them, and screams and prayers were silenced by massive jaws and ripping claws. I found myself praying out loud for the heroic heart of our Lord and the courageous dedication of those who belonged to the daring young church.

II

What then must you do if Christ is to become real in your life and if you are to thrillingly share the Gospel's life-changing message?

First, let Jesus receive you. Religion at its best is simply this: the giving of one's self in utter abandonment to Christ.

Jesus said that we could not serve God and mammon. If I were allowed to get across only one point to you it would be this: the real joy, the actual experience of complete Christianity can only be known and shared when, in your heart of hearts, you give everything to him. There must

34

not be one room kept locked, one closet kept guarded, one key kept hidden. For this not only forbids Christ's spirit to come in his fullness but it means that you may actually convince yourself that this sheltered darkness does not really need the light. You may feel that what is wrong for others is not so bad for you. Therefore, sin loses its terror. By such a process of rationalization, though the world may look upon you as a fairly decent chap, your own inner nature will be wasting away. For whenever you seek his companionship or guidance or strength, you will hear the tender yet uncompromising voice of the Master who demands all, saying, "One thing thou lackest." The tragedy is not only that you miss the spiritual power but that you say, almost with a bit of pride, since I only lack one thing I am very much better than my neighbor who is possessed with the legion. Yet, conscious of that one sin, you may be further from the main highway than the worst of demoniacs.

We must remember too that there is no once and for all business in the life of a Christian. However full your heart has been today with the presence of the Savior, tomorrow you must again lean upon him in complete confidence. Evil takes no vacation in its conquest of the soul. Each morning you must trust his companionship to help you and believe that his power can keep you. Complete consecration is daily consecration. I once had a teacher who said that he could see a man in the gutter and think were it not for the grace of God he could have been as that man.

But he also added that were it not for the grace of God he could still be as that man.

After you have let Jesus receive you, let him remake you. Moody used to tell his congregations to give themselves to Christ because God could do more with their lives than they could.

When Jeremiah went to the potter's house he saw that the vessel being made was spoiled. Then what did the potter do? I like Moffatt's translation: "He re-moulded it to please himself, till he was satisfied." God does not turn us down or cast us away. He wants to make us complete and without blemish. If we will but allow him, he will remold us until he is satisfied. And although his complete satisfaction may depend upon our complete perfection, he is pleased with any progress we make along the trail. To me this is the most thrilling thing in the world: what we can become if we hold fast to our Lord. It may not be until we stand within the gates of the heavenly city that his perfection will possess us, but we have the eternal promise that we shall some day be like him.

The risk is great. The cause is demanding. Even your closest friends may say that you are carrying religion too far. But the truth is that religion will be carrying you ever upward and onward. Only heaven is the limit when you enter God's pottery shop.

But not only must you allow him to receive you and remake you, you must let Jesus send you out. This was the experience of Zaccheus. After he had received Christ and been given a new reason for living, he put this new life to work. He gave half of all he possessed to the poor and began looking for anyone he had wronged.

Remember the half-man, half-beast from Gadara. Not only had he been bound with chains but perhaps even worse he was completely ignored and left alone. Then Jesus touched him, and this devil-possessed man became a God-possessed preacher and was appointed an apostle to his countrymen.

After Christ comes in your life and wonderfully changes things, you will want to testify that it is true. And make no mistake about it, your testimony counts for much. The little girl who said, "Since Jesus came, I feel all clean inside," can share her heart's purity with others. The wash-woman E. Stanley Jones tells about, who exclaimed, "I ain't what I ought to be and I ain't what I'm gonna be, but I'm heap better than I used to be," can tell the people how it is that she is different.[2] And Dale Evans Rogers who witnessed, "I looked for my pot of gold at the foot of the rainbow and found it at the foot of the Cross," has already told many thousands of what Calvary has done for her. You will never know until God wills it how much your life has meant and how much your witness has helped.

Again, it will not be easy. Christ promised a great life but he also promised Gethsemanes and Golgothas. There is the

[2] From *How to Be a Transformed Person.*

promise of a crown, but never without the certainty of a cross. The one way to life glorified is along the road of self-crucified. Yet the reward far outshines the sacrifice as the morning sun does the midnight sky. There is the promise of his presence and the joy of being used to win others to the life eternal.

CHAPTER FOUR

Repentance

"Thus it is written . . . that repentance . . . should be preached in his name."—Luke 24:46-47

• The Gospel of Luke might be called the Gospel of Hope. In its pages we find many instances of new life that repentance brings. Over and over we see thrilling proofs of the regeneration that our Lord gave when some hungry soul beaten by the world or defeated by personal sin came to him eager for a fresh beginning. The tender and loving heart of the Savior like a latchstring stayed constantly accessible to the man who wanted to start anew.

Yet more than an accessible heart, it is a searching love that goes into the hills after a lamb or into the corners after a coin. It is not even his servants but the Master himself seeking and urging the lost ones to come home.

Though these messages are centered on the theme of our desire for God, we must be aware that ever and always God is taking the initiative. Though it is true to say that in

Christ we find God, "it is perhaps even more true," says Paul Scherer, "that in Christ God finds us."

And so there is little point in even beginning the search for truth unless we are captivated by the assurance that our blessed Lord, himself the truth, is doing everything within his power this very moment to make us conscious of his reality and to forgive, strengthen, and guide. More than we could ever possibly want life that is abundant, he wants to give it to us at its radiant best. And although these messages deal in the main with our attitude toward Calvary and what has already been done for us, it is imperative that we understand that the Holy Spirit is doing everything possible from hour to hour to cause repentance and to make us God conscious.

With this in mind, let us ask ourselves how we can become conscious of his presence; how can we know real repentance?

I

Let us see what repentance is not.

It is not an emotional outburst. Now, to be sure, there will be some very real and very deep emotional feeling concerning our attitude toward the way. This is certainly not a study of the problem of emotional behavior, but two points should be made very clear.

First, we have strong feeling about so much else. If we become excited about war, politics, illness, even a motion picture with a touching plot, it would seem we should

40

be moved concerning the Savior who is able to do exceeding abundantly above all that we ask or think, whether it be in the realm of world affairs or the deep longings of the heart. The second point follows closely. Religion is not just emotion. Having strong feeling about God should lead straight into complete dedication to God. To be valid your experience should not only include the excitement of entering the gate but your willingness to walk the road. It is true that religion is caught, but little good is done unless it is kept.

Consider Luke's stories of two men who had "emotional" experiences. One is recorded in his Gospel, the other in the Acts. How widely blind Bartimaeus and Simon the Magician differed. Bartimaeus came hungry for healing; Simon followed searching for sensation. Bartimaeus offered himself; Simon, his money. Bartimaeus was cured; Simon was rebuked. Yet Luke tells us that Simon believed. Now this indicates that he was converted, but the desire for personal notoriety robbed him of the witness he might have given; hence, he simply lost his experience, the only way one can ever lose his experience, by not being willing to keep it. Bartimaeus not only received his sight but when we last see him, he is following, glorifying Christ. An emotional experience should lead from receiving to following and glorifying.

Repentance is not self-abasement. Paul told the Corinthians that they were temples of God. This in no way contradicts the giving of one's self, for there is all the difference

41

in the world between self-abasement and self-giving. You are to hold yourself in high regard and with great respect.

The author of the eighth psalm says, "Thou hast made him (man) a little lower than the angels." The Revised Standard Version translates in a far better way: "Thou hast made him little less than God." You are not a worm groveling in the dust. You are to mount up with wings like the eagle. You are made in God's image. Of course you may mar that image, preferring a worm's crawl to an eagle's wing. It is easy to be anchored down by things which self desires when it is so needful that you yearn with all your being for the God-self, which is the true self, Christ in you. So when Samuel Johnson writes, "My chief vocation in life is trying to escape from myself," the answer is that this is possible in the spiritual realm only when we allow Jesus' higher self entrance and perfect right of way.

Then repentance is not simply sadness over sin. Repentance involves certainly sorrow for past sins, failures, and faults. But it must never stop here. Real repentance does not leave you in the pigpen mourning; it always leads you to the Father's house rejoicing. The younger son did more than come to himself. He did more than resolve to arise. He left the swine and returned to the waiting arms of the one who loved him. Judas failed at this point. Though brokenhearted, he yet refused to seek him who would have pardoned even from the cross. Peter's denial was nearly as cutting as Judas' betrayal; yet through his tears he found the forgiveness of a merciful Lord. The difference was that Judas regretted and sought death; Peter repented and found life. Judas went out; Peter went back. Repentance is a sorrow for, but always a surrender to.

I am thinking of a man who is one of the most victorious Christians I know. After years of folly and failure, he permitted Christ to enter his heart. The abundant life began in his living room when he faced the men who had come out of love to see him and said, "Right here I'm through with sin. I'm giving up to God." He was sorry for his sins but repentant enough to surrender to God and quit them.

II

Now, to be positive, repentance is a change of purpose. Consider Paul. His intent was to oppress and punish. Then he met Jesus and it became the determination of his soul to introduce everyone to his new friend. Paul had been sincere in his attempt at destroying the followers of the way, but a light, a voice, a command, and his response led the man of Tarsus to an entirely new reason for living. When you repent, your plans are changed and you let God take supreme command.

A great life is made possible only by a great purpose. We read in the fifth chapter of Acts that the disciples left the Jewish council "rejoicing that they were counted worthy to suffer dishonor for the name." Why was this? Earlier they had been the church with the fearful heart and trembling hand. They had followed at a distance; most of them had not even followed at all. What had happened? "Every day in the temple and at home they did not cease teaching and preaching Jesus." Their living Lord gave them a big purpose. We can face anything, indeed all things, if the reason be great enough.

In the second place repentance is a dedication of heart. When speaking to one seeking new life in Christ, I used to question him at great length concerning the sin problem and anxiously suggest wholehearted confession. In some situations this is still necessary. In most instances however the extent of our dedication does not depend upon how many of our sins we are willing to confess, but how much of ourselves we are willing to consecrate. A youthful disciple, pledging his devotion, prayed, "Lord Jesus, I take hands off, as far as my life is concerned. I put thee on the throne in my heart. Change, cleanse, use me as thou shalt choose. I take the full power of thy Holy Spirit." [1] That is repentance; not shallow and superficial, but devoted and deep.

Possibly our greatest hymn is:

> My faith looks up to Thee
> Thou Lamb of Calvary,
> Saviour divine!
> Now hear me while I pray,
> Take all my guilt away,
> O let me from this day
> Be wholly Thine!

[1] *Borden of Yale.*

Finally, repentance is a pathway of obedience. No man ever wandered away from God who did not first fail at this point. Every sin stems from disobedience to the will of God. When someone asks which is the greatest sin, I always answer not obeying God. Every man who ever received the death sentence, every person guilty of evils against society, every unarrested criminal who walks the streets with crime in his heart, every stumbling-block church member who may even attend church occasionally and yet has no compassion for his neighbor has reached his particular place by disobeying Christ. God calls every man to some specific task, some particular assignment. Of course some of us do not seek his will for our lives and we adopt our own policies quite confident that we know what is best. Others know that God has a plan for them, but they have plans of their own.

A man who has started the last lap of the journey confessed to me recently that when a boy, he had been called to preach. He admitted sadly that he had never known full happiness because he had resisted God's summons. It is true, as I explained to him, that he has made a very definite contribution both as a Christian father to his children and a helpful layman in his church. Yet the heartbreak of inner rebellion testified to me, as I have found in so many other cases, nothing can overcome one's disobedience to Christ.

Isaiah said that the willing and obedient are those who enjoy the good things of God, and Jonah found as did the poet centuries later that "in His will there is peace."

The vision on the Damascus road got Paul's attention; obedience to the vision got Paul. He could have seen Christ and turned his own way. The rich young man did. "I was not disobedient to the heavenly vision" helped build the church and start the world-wide witness. It will work today if we are willing.

CHAPTER FIVE

Forgiveness

"But the tax collector, standing far off, would not even lift up his eyes to heaven, but beat his breast, saying, 'God, be merciful to me a sinner!'" —Luke 18:13 (R.S.V.)

• When man with complete surrender in his heart repents, then God with infinite love in his heart forgives. Perhaps more than any other Gospel, Luke emphasizes repentance. This is true also with regard to forgiveness.

Two men went into the temple to pray and all similarity ends there. They were alike in where they went but not why they went. They were not alike in what happened when they arrived. And when they left, the difference in their hearts was as great as a drop of dew and the Atlantic Ocean.

The Pharisee was proud; the tax collector was humble. The Pharisee bragged on himself; the tax collector confessed he was a sinner. The Pharisee was rebuked; the tax collector went out forgiven, having received God's mercy. To experience the forgiveness of God, we must come to him humbly, willing to confess our sins and accept his pardon.

I

The tax collector came humbly to church seeking the presence of God.

There is a story in the Old Testament about a splendid young man, long on nobility but short on grace, who entered the temple one day. In one of the great prophetic chapters of the Bible we see the actual making of the young prophet, Isaiah. But it was not the seraphim nor the vibrating foundations nor the smoke filled sanctuary that made the youthful aristocrat see himself as lost and unclean. Hear his testimony: "Mine eyes have seen the King, the Lord of hosts." Regardless of a man's aristocracy, environment, or position, when he sees the king the walls of self-esteem crumble.

Now when you think of Christ, and particularly about his death, you certainly realize your own worth. Possibly the reason the centurion cried out at Calvary that here was a son of God was because he had been changed by taking a long look at the dying Redeemer. A continued gaze at the cross will not only impress upon you who he was but also what you may become. But your worth and possibilities should take a back seat to your deep feeling of unworthiness and failure and sin when you first look at the king. Indeed, conviction of sin precedes conversion to grace. A proud man never sees himself as a sinner. A humble seeker sees nothing else. The Pharisee saw only how much better he was than his associate. The publican saw only how much less he was than his Lord. The result was that one came down with a pious expression while the other came down with a purifying experience.

We must not close our eyes to the ugliness of man's inner condition apart from God. James Stewart reminds us that when sin has been rationalized away, forgiveness will always appear unnecessary and irrelevant. How true this is. If we say that sin is not so bad, we are saying at the same time that forgiveness is not so good. So often we miss the joy of the radiant relationship with One who washes whiter than snow for our proud hearts do not admit that they are unclean.

An American traveling in England sought out an old friend living in a rural section. As he entered the yard, he noticed the clean wash hanging from the line. Coming from an industrial city where smoke and smog prevailed, he was amazed at the whiteness of the wash. While he sat in the house, a light snow fell. On walking out and gazing at the immaculate hillside bedecked in snowflakes, he exclaimed that the wash did not now appear to be as white as before. The elderly woman, who had been his hostess, answered with a penetrating poignancy, "Aye, but what can look white when it is beside God Almighty's white?"

The tax collector confessed his sin to God.

While I was in seminary it was my privilege to study systematic theology under Claude Thompson. I remember one day as he was discussing forgiveness, a student inter-

49

rupted with, "Doctor, which is the sin God will not forgive?"

Quickly came his answer, "The sin you will not confess."

In Hawthorne's great novel, *The Scarlet Letter*, we see
the tragedy of failure to confess. Arthur Dimmesdale, the
brilliant young minister, and Hester Prynne, who was mar-
ried to another, engaged in that most sacred of all in-
timacies. A baby girl born to Hester revealed her sin. She
was forced to wear the letter "A" made out of bright red
cloth for all the town people to see. No one suspected the
highly regarded minister. But day after day, Arthur Dimmesdale wasted away in the solitary confinement of his own
guilt. He withheld his confession. Better to wear the Scarlet
Letter on your cloak than to have it engraved on your heart.

Remember too that confession must be from the heart.
There may be cheeks wet with tears but the important
thing is for the heart to be truly repentant.

After denying his Lord, Peter's repentance brought
cleansing. After betraying his Lord, Judas' regret brought
suicide. Confession to God with the heart grieved for wrong-
doing releases you from sin's guilt and opens the door to
God's grace.

In order that forgiveness be complete there must be acceptance. We read, "He went to his house justified." Jesus
would never have said that had the tax collector not received forgiveness. God is more willing to give than you are
to take. Christ's hands are outstretched offering pardon. For

you to experience the peace forgiveness brings, your hands must be outstretched to receive it.

When Bartimaeus reached out in the dark toward Jesus, he did not ask that he be allowed to earn his eyesight. He did not offer what little was in his beggar's cup for the priceless privilege of seeing. He said, "Lord, let me receive my sight." What vision is to the eye, forgiveness is to the heart. Receiving this experience gives you spiritual perception and inward peace that nothing else brings. When you pray, "Come, Thou Fount of every blessing," the streams of mercy begin their cleansing flow.

Take, receive, and accept were the words that Jesus used when he gave his kingdom invitation. They are the pathways to forgiveness and to God's fullness.

II

What will forgiveness do in your life when you receive it?

First forgiveness pardons the failure of yesterday. A man once said the tragedy of his life was that he had given his strength to secondary things. The unimportant had been given priority over the important; the minor was on the throne and the major in the dust. Now this need not have led him to despair. Should you make this same discovery the realization that you have made a muddle of life can lead you into the arms of Jesus. Forget the days that have passed. God wants your energy for daring enterprises and spiritual conquests.

As Nathan convicted the soul of David, the king wept inwardly realizing the way he had betrayed God. He remembered when as a shepherd boy he had walked beside still waters and rested in green pastures conscious of the reality of God. He thought of the times when after weary days of fighting, he had found refuge and repose in the Lord. He recalled that during times of strife with Saul or days of loneliness apart from Jonathan God had been with him to strengthen and sustain. He longed for the restoration of the joy of salvation he had once known. And so he prayed for a clean heart and a steadfast spirit that once again he could know and share the Divine Presence.

Paul knew he had broken God's heart by molesting and persecuting the Christians. He felt his ministry to have been a failure at Athens. Yet he knew too of the forgiving spirit of his Lord and he told the Philippians that he was putting the past out of his mind and answering the upward call.

Former days may bring bitter recollections, but God wants you to be miserable no longer. He is willing to forget your yesterdays and he says so. Before victorious living is yours, you must forget them too.

A few days ago I talked with a young woman who anxiously desired to be a Christian. But selfish passion had so long pushed to the background the yearning for Christ she doubted if her stunted soul could rise. We knelt and asked the lifting Lord to draw her to himself. When she rose from her knees not only had the Lord forgiven her but in his love she had forgiven herself.

Forgiveness purifies the intentions for today. New life brings with it new resolution and the fixed purpose of our hearts is now to be about our Father's business. Our greatest aim is to render any service we can for his sake.

When the woman washed the feet of Jesus, he did not question her sincerity. He knew her motive. She had been freshly forgiven and her gratitude had to be expressed. Therefore, what was ordinarily an act of bondage became an expression of love. For some people any kindness toward their fellows would be sheer drudgery. Then they give their lives to Christ, are forgiven, and their burdensome tasks become joyful privileges.

Washing dishes will be less monotonous when family love becomes the heart's aim. Attending church could be a delight instead of a duty if the motive were right. Knocking on doors and being a personal ambassador for Christ is not so much a requirement for discipleship as it is a result of forgiveness. Being pardoned enables a man to do a complete about-face in thought and action.

I am thinking of a layman whom I trust and love deeply. He had grown cold in the faith and his testimony held for little in the community. Then one night he recognized the failure of selfishness and grasped the hand of his Savior. He asked for forgiveness which Christ had been seeking to grant. He became a new man and in his soul burned a new fire. I have visited and walked the roads with him

53

often and many times have been strengthened by his witness.

Finally, forgiveness protects the consecration of tomorrow. Until you accepted Christ's pardon, the only thing you were committed to was being uncommitted. Your part is to give willingness; Christ's part is to give wholeness. Your responsibility is to give self; Christ's responsibility is to give strength. When God takes possession of a life, his power enters and fortifies the soul against temptation. Forgiveness enables you to see that you are no longer alone when the storms swell and the billows break. Christ has redeemed the past. He has given the present life new meaning. And his everlasting arms are undergirding you now so that you can look toward tomorrow confidently. Under his banner you, like Browning, can be

> One who never turned his back but marched breast
> forward,
> Never doubted clouds would break,
> Never dreamed though right were worsted
> wrong would triumph.

Several years ago I was preaching in a fine Presbyterian school. At the conclusion of the service the president of the student council came to me and said, "I agreed with everything you said today. I would like very much to be a Christian but I do not think I have the courage to live the Christian life." This young man was extremely earnest so I said, "Don, if Jesus through God's power could push a

54

stone away from his grave and walk out alive forevermore, don't you believe he could push the sin out of your life and keep it pushed out?"

He thought a moment; then he said, "I never thought of it that way before. Yes, I do believe that, and by the help of God, I will let him do it in my life." It is only when forgiveness comes in that such faith can hold out.

Perhaps you have thought that you would be unable to stand firm should you accept Christ's offer. You thought right. But he will not let your foot be moved. Christ himself will do the holding if you do the consenting. He only waits for you to say you need him.

Do you remember the woman who had been caught in adultery and brought by the scribes and Pharisees to Jesus? They told him of the woman's sin and reminded him of Moses' command to stone such who were found. They thought they had him. If he spoke in her behalf they would have said he disagreed with Mosaic law. If he spoke against her the emphasis in his gospel would be no longer redemption but retribution. He answered, "He that is without sin among you, let him first cast a stone at her."

But the important thing to remember here is this. After her accusers had gone, Jesus said, "Go, and sin no more." During those few moments of agony and embarrassment the pity, compassion, and forgiveness of Jesus had made her a new woman. It was not his condemnation but his courageous faith that pointed her to a future without fear. This can be God's certainty for your life.

CHAPTER SIX

Conversion

"But Saul, still breathing threats and murder against the disciples of the Lord, went to the high priest and asked him for letters to the synagogues at Damascus, so that if he found any belonging to the Way, men or women, he might bring them bound to Jerusalem."—Acts 9:1-2 (R.S.V.)

"And Paul said, . . . 'I would to God that . . . all who hear me this day might become such as I am.'"
—Acts 26:29 (R.S.V.)

• There is a chasm dividing these portions of scripture. On one hand we see a man terrorizing and threatening. On the other, we see a man preaching and proclaiming. On one side of the chasm we see a Jewish persecutor destroying those who belonged to the way. We look to the opposite side and see a missionary-evangelist desiring the whole world to have what he has found in Christ. The first reading concerns a man who laid waste the Church and entered house after house, dragging off men and women and committing them to prison. The second selection tells of a man who laid waste the forces of darkness, and entering city after city, thrilled the multitudes with the testimony of his risen Lord and committed them to God. On his way to Damascus, we see Saul. Standing behind bars at Caesarea, we meet Paul. Realizing the great gulf fixed, we wonder what has happened to this man.

When Jesus had removed the unclean spirits from the demoniac, he charged him to go and tell of his release. Mark then relates that this liberated man went home to proclaim how much the Lord had done for him.

So it was with Paul. On the Damascus road he saw Christ; and obeying that vision, declared to Jew and Gentile that they should turn to God. This is true conversion—an encounter with Christ and obedience to him.

I

The man seeking conversion is entirely dependent upon God's saving grace.

One of the most often quoted definitions of grace is that it is unmerited love, meaning simply that we don't deserve it. Many people miss the new birth here. This is a work-for-what-you-get civilization. The necessities we have and the luxuries we enjoy are ours because toil has earned them. But God so loved that he gave. Salvation can be ours not because of what we accomplish but what we accept. The apostle whose life was so radically changed by admitting grace into his heart said, "This is not your own doing, it is the gift of God." And so we do not work to get

57

it, but we do work to keep it if by work we mean having steadfast hearts which die daily to self. Good works and pure deeds are the result, never the cause of salvation.

John Henry Jowett said that grace is God in action. I have always liked that. I think it is exactly what Paul meant in his letter to the church at Ephesus. How Paul loved to proclaim the gospel of grace! He desired the Roman church to receive an abundance of it. He reminded the Corinthian church what knowledge of it had done for men. He besought the Galatian church to return to it. To those whom he wrote, Paul considered it more than a benediction closing an epistle. It became their only strength during days of imprisonment and persecution. As men and women faced dungeon cells and fiery brands their one hope and help was, "The grace of the Lord Jesus be with you." Paul was thus able to give courage to thousands because he had allowed God to take action in his life.

If grace is the one way to becoming Christian, it is also the means of keeping Christian. The New Testament admonishes us to maintain the spiritual glow and to grow in grace. When we find ourselves strangely ineffective as a church in our modern world, it is because we have allowed the glow to fade and the grace to die. Though Bernard of Clairvaux wrote these words over eight hundred years ago, they need to be unceasingly proclaimed:

Ask but His grace, and lo, 'tis given!
Ask, and He turns your hell to heaven:

Though sin and sorrow wound my soul,
Jesus, Thy balm will make it whole.

I think there comes a time in every man's life when he must needs go back to something. It occurs to me that during difficult days and harrowing nights Paul must have journeyed in memory back to the Damascus road, back to the time when he first received redeeming grace. Doubts constantly renew their attack on the soul; and who has not known those anxious times when unbelief sought to purge us of our passion? Indeed at times great conviction comes only as we strive to walk up from valleys.

Frederick W. Robertson knew that faith which is victorious comes hard. His body was frail and weak with affliction. And yet the painful pathway upon which the great preacher of Brighton walked led at last to such intimacy with his Lord as he never dreamed could exist. In returning to faith's great moments he found victory over depression's blue moments. I often pray, as did a friend of mine, "Oh God, help me to remember those moments when I have been most aware of thy presence." Then I return in my memory to those experiences of certainty—although he is ever present if I am but willing through faith's eyes to see.

Grace is able in all circumstances. When Paul besought the Lord concerning the thorn in his flesh, he received this answer, "My grace is sufficient for you." Looking back over the days of insults and calamities, this sufficiency enabled him to say, "I am content with . . . hardships . . . for when I am weak, then I am strong." Paul found that the grace of Christ was not only saving but sustaining.

II

One seeking to meet God trusts not only in his saving grace but in his divine love.

Before his conversion, Paul had been in strict subservience to the law. Then he met Christ, and we listen as he says that he has found a more excellent way. What the law could not do, God through Christ could. This was the grand orchestra he directed. This was the gospel he proclaimed. "The greatest of these is love," was more than a statement of ethics sent to Corinth; it was the testimony of Paul's heart directed to all men. There is no truer indication of real conversion than this: a man is a lover instead of a hater. It was his hatred of the interference of these upstart young Christians that had led Paul to Damascus. But now it was his love for his risen Lord that lifted him above Jewish authority and led him across the Western world. That same love is available today. The more excellent way still leads to joyous living and victorious witnessing.

Some years ago I was helping in an evangelistic endeavor in Malaya. My last days of preaching were in the mountain cities many miles above Singapore. I shall never forget the final service in one of these cities. A short while before the hour of worship, a youthful Malayan lad came to see me at the missionary home where I was staying. He reminded me

60

that he was one of the group that had answered the invitation to accept Christ two evenings before. He wondered if I would give him an opportunity that night to tell the congregation what Jesus Christ had done for him. I remember thinking to myself that this boy had only been a Christian two days. I was not sure he knew enough about Christ to give such a testimony. So I put him off by saying that the service had already been thoroughly planned but that if I should need assistance I would send for him.

I preached to the filled church that night about the change that Jesus makes in the hearts of those who will yield to him. I invited any who were willing to deny self, take up the cross, and follow him, to come forward. There was some response, but not that for which we had hoped and prayed. Suddenly I felt a vigorous tugging at my coat, and there he stood, looking for all the world like a runner about to start the hundred-yard dash. With a glow in his eyes and a tremendous excitement in his voice, he asked, "May I tell them now?"

Who could have said no under such circumstances? And so I answered, "Now."

I do not recall ever viewing such a scene as the one that followed. The lad spoke very calmly and yet with a blessed assurance: "The Buddha never answered a prayer and never gave me cause for joy or happiness; but these last two days Jesus Christ has so filled my heart that I can never possibly want anything else but him." Then very softly he concluded, "What he has done for me, he will do for you if you will trust him."

I stood and watched Pentecost received again. When the seekers quit coming, there was no room left to kneel or stand. And I thought I was not going to allow that boy to speak for I had not felt that he could know enough of the Savior to share. I don't suppose that the light flashed for more than two minutes that day on the highway to Damascus, but God is not limited in the length of time that it takes for him to lead a man home. Divine love can do in two seconds what man's will allows. It is only as we allow his love to enter our lives and govern our actions that we can understand conversion. This is the greatest evidence of a transformed life—a heart that is filled with the love Christ gives. Jesus said that this was the disciple's mark of distinction.

He did not say the world would recognize you as his follower because of any doctrine which you sanctioned or the mode of worship you practiced. He did not say you would be recognized by any particular group affiliation. But it is love that reveals your true identity. It is love that proves you are united with the Master.

> I've found a Friend, O such a Friend!
>   He loved me ere I knew Him;
> He drew me with the cords of love,
>   And thus He bound me to Him.

62

Paul's life revealing God's love assured the world that what he said had happened on the Damascus road was true.

III

Because of God's saving grace and divine love, conversion is possible. For conversion to be complete and lasting, one must give faithful witness to it.

Paul was not being boastful when he said to Agrippa, "I would to God that all who hear me this day might become as I am." He was obeying the heavenly vision. These words expressed the deep longing of his soul for all who heard his message to know the One about whom he spoke. Such faithful witnessing was stirring to the listener and rewarding to the kingdom. Even those who hated him admitted he had turned the world upside down.

Hear him as he preaches to the Ephesian elders at Miletus: "And now, behold, I go bound in the spirit unto Jerusalem, not knowing the things that shall befall me there: Save that the Holy Ghost witnesseth in every city, saying that bonds and afflictions abide me. But none of these things move me, neither count I my life dear unto myself, so that I might finish my course with joy, and the ministry, which I have received of the Lord Jesus, to testify the gospel of the grace of God." And when he finished speaking the people wept unashamedly as they embraced him, their hearts broken because of the realization that they should not see his face again. Men do not behave in such fashion unless they have been deeply stirred. They do not

63

act in such a way unless they have been sitting at the feet of one, who like Jesus shed tears of love and pity for those who are as sheep that have no shepherd.

And so in this hour of deliberate sin and desperate need, the Lord still speaks to his servants, telling us to go out into the highways and hedges and compel the lost to come in, that his house may be filled. If we are converted we will obey. It may be that those so far from the Father's house may never draw near unless Christ be recognized by the sweet persuasiveness in the lives of his servants whom he has sent.

Emerson, speaking before a college audience, once said, "It is the office of a true teacher to show that God is, not was; that He speaketh, not spake." Has Christ become real in your life: does he speak through your lips?

In many instances we will not even have to "go out." We will be brought face to face with opportunities surrounding us.

Recently while I was preaching in one of our southern cities, a little girl came to the front to shake hands with me at the conclusion of a service. Her older sister standing by kept urging her to tell me something, but she was a bit hesitant. Finally, rather shyly and not the slightest boastfully, she told me of an incident which had occurred the day before. A woman visiting in that city from a distant state, attempting to place a telephone call, had rung the little girl's phone by mistake. Though it was the wrong number, the child began to talk to the woman. Remembering the services which were being held at her church, she invited the stranger to attend that evening. The woman replied that she had not been inside a church for twenty years. The girl told her of the church's location and urged her to come. Then the little girl, who had lost all trace of timidity in the wonder of this experience, said with an excited joy, "She was at church tonight and when you gave the invitation to surrender to Jesus, she was one of those who came forward." The woman dialed the right number. She had talked with a youthful disciple who was loyal in her witness for Christ.

The disciples at first doubted that Paul had passed from death unto life. What convinced them? Barnabas tells us that it was his boldness as he spoke in the name of the Lord. Such a witness with your lips and life will convince the world that you too have met the Master.

CHAPTER SEVEN

Friendship with Christ

"No longer do I call you servants, for the servant does not know what his master is doing; but I have called you friends, for all that I have heard from my Father I have made known to you."—John 15:15 (R.S.V.)

• The converted man is a changed man because he has allowed the divine friend to take entire possession of his life. Here in John's Gospel Jesus is telling about the union that exists when one belongs to him. Master and servant share no intimacy, know nothing in common, he says. But my relationship to you is that of friend with friend.

Now Jesus told the disciples that he had called them, and again, that he had chosen them. He wanted to be their friend. It is his desire to be our friend. He is the one that makes the offer. His is the wish for two hearts to share this tie that binds. This is the very soul of the gospel; not that we love God but that he loves us. The idea, he has. The offer, he presents. The initiative, he takes. His divine presence, he gladly gives.

66

Later messages deal with how this friendship may grow eternally more beautiful. But our main regard here is what his divine affection will do in each of our lives. He lived his friendship in life. He proved his friendship in death. And now alive forevermore, the eternal friend offers his friendship to us.

I

His friendship is ever lifting.

If a man is down, he needs to be lifted up. Of all the vanities that the preacher in Ecclesiastes woefully bemoans, I think I sympathize more with the man who falls and has not another to lift him up. But this need not be the case. There is a hand that raises. There is a heart that redeems.

Not long ago I visited one just a few steps from the end of the trail. He had cancer of the spine. Years before he had killed a man and he could not fathom the truth that the Savior would forgive him. With a desperate earnestness and yet an unspeakable wistfulness, he asked, "Will Jesus take a man like me?"

I told him that Christ stood even at his bedside yearning to grant him heaven's friendship. "His word reminds us," I told him, "that he is faithful and will forgive our sins and cleanse us from all unrighteousness if we will but open the heart's door." When I left his room he still had cancer of the spine, but he no longer had cancer of the soul.

Of course if a man is up, he can always be lifted higher. I remember hearing Stanley Jones tell about a question that a little girl asked him. The query was if he had ever wanted anything he didn't have. The missionary said he had never been asked that question before, but after thinking a moment he replied that he just wanted more of what he had. Well, so do I. And every sincere Christian is eager to be lifted higher and intent upon that friendship becoming stronger.

Elisha was by no means the man Elijah was, but he became a power because of his association with his friend. When Elijah left him, Elisha's last request was for a double share of his spirit.

David spent a great deal of time hiding and fleeing from Saul. I think he might have turned bitter and never had the spirit to become the man after God's own heart had he not had a beautiful friendship. Jonathan was a right arm to him always, and the book of Samuel tells us that he loved him as he loved his own soul.

There was awkward, talkative Peter. Here for a moment, gone the next. Devoted one instant, denying a few hours later. But he had a friend who kept praying for strength to come and faith to hold. That friendship gradually did its blessed work and Simon was changed from a reed to a rock.

II

His friendship is ever faithful.

Hidden away in the book of II Kings there is a thrilling little story. The king of Syria was besieging Dothan. He had a great army that came by night and surrounded the city.

When Elisha's servant saw that army, he was panic stricken. "What shall we do?" he nervously questioned.

Elisha answered, "Fear not, for those who are with us are more than those who are with them." Then Elisha prayed, "O Lord, I pray thee, open his eyes that he may see." And the Lord did open his eyes, "and behold, the mountain was full of horses and chariots of fire round about Elisha." They were not alone. And neither are you. The eternal God is your dwelling place and underneath are the everlasting arms. You have a friend who is constantly beside you and who will not fail you.

Moses told the struggling Israelites to be strong and of good courage; the Lord their God would go before them and he would not fail them nor forsake them. He knew that by experience. Possibly even as he offered them this assurance, he was remembering himself as a fearful, hesitant young man who long ago presented the Lord with excuses why he should not be commander of his people. But the Lord had promised to walk beside him, and somehow in the strength of that friendship, Pharaohs and Red Seas and murmurings and enemies were only shadows through which the sunlight of God could shine.

A later sermon treats of the urgent need for prayer, the soul's grandest avenue into the presence of God. We say that God does not always answer our requests, but that he most certainly meets our needs. God gives us, through friendship with Christ, the faith and strength to turn life's dark corners with certainty. That does not mean that he fulfills every wish, that he saves from every snare. But it does mean that his presence never forsakes us. It means that the man who clings to Christ, who depends upon his friendship, is inwardly fortified to face any difficulty with confidence and hope.

We don't use this hymn often but it is a good one to sing and pray constantly:

> O Holy Saviour, Friend unseen,
> Since on Thine arm Thou bidd'st me lean,
> Help me, through-out life's changing scene,
>   By faith to cling to Thee.
>
> What tho' the world deceitful prove,
> And earthly friends and hopes remove;
> With patient, uncomplaining love,
>   Still, would I cling to Thee.
>
> Though oft I seem to tread alone
> Life's dreary waste, with thorns o'ergrown,
> Thy voice of love, in gentlest tone,
>   Still whispers, "Cling to me!"
>
> Though faith and hope may long be tried,
> I ask not, need not, aught beside;
> How safe, how calm, how satisfied,
>   The soul that clings to Thee.

The Lord constantly reaches down bidding us grasp his hand. The reason we have not felt that divine energy permeating our spirits is because we have not reached up and received. He is a searching Savior, but so often we are not even seeking sinners. Our lives have become nothing more than minus signs. I know of no worse hell than to be satiated with self, satisfied to be a sinner.

Now and then I talk to a man who says, "I'm not a hypocrite. I sin in public. I don't run around and hide when I do my meanness." I have never understood why he would think that was an indication of merit. He says he is an honest sinner. I say there is no such thing. He is a complacent sinner. He is a man that is as close to damnation as one can get. He doesn't blush when he curses. He is not embarrassed when someone detects the smell of liquor on his breath.

When I was a small boy, I slipped away from home a few times to smoke. Of course, fear of punishment was one reason for hiding. But the main reason was that my mother had taught me that it was wrong for little chaps to smoke, and I had promised her I wouldn't. I did not want to betray her confidence in me. My conscience bothered me for what I was doing and I soon quit. When one becomes ashamed of the way he is living, he is not far from the kingdom.

Bring your guilt and your shame and your embarrassed heart to the friend who understands and receives and pardons your transgressions. He has not failed to seek you. You can risk your life on his promise that "him who comes to me I will not cast out," he will not fail to save you.

III

His friendship is ever growing.

When the steward of the feast tasted the wine that Jesus had changed from water, he said, "You have kept the good wine until now." This is ever and always true with his beautiful friendship. When I first accepted this glorious gift, I was thrilled and happy and excited. His touch completely and permanently changed my life. Years have passed since as a wayward, selfish boy, I knelt quietly in a room and told the Lord I wanted to be his friend. The friendship becomes dearer each time I seek his presence. It grows sweeter every day. It is adventure unlimited and joy beyond description.

I believe strongly in complete consecration. Purity of heart is the desire of each of God's friends. As we walk with him, imperfections in our lives will be noticed. Time spent in intimate communion will reveal this to us.

I have a friend that I love dearly. I think he is the kindest, most Christlike soul that I have ever known. We have spent many days together and though God's mission for his life has taken him half-a-world away, the memory of our past experiences gives me renewed strength and dedication each time I think about them. Christ fairly shines in his every act of unselfish service. My own flaws and failings seemed never so prominent as when I walked with him. Many times after leaving him I have quietly promised God I would be a better man. It is infinitely more so with our Master. The more we seek his face, the longer we hold his hand, we will see the little things we have done and the little creatures we have been. We will promise with Paul not to nullify but to realize and receive his grace.

It does not take long for a baby to be born. But it takes years for him to learn how to respond to life and become adjusted to the great world about him. The new birth can come into a heart in a second. But I have found that for most of God's children it takes patience and discipline and often disappointments and heartaches before a man can say with certainty that he belongs completely to God. It may not be until we stand together in that fair homeland that we shall know all the delights of his love. But I do know this. As we live with our Friend and introduce him to others, we shall become more and more like him. And the great dream of our lives shall be for a friendship ever closer and dearer.

It was said of James Denney, the beloved Scotch preacher, that during his later years he could not even speak the name of Jesus without being deeply moved. Friendship with the Master filled his life with increased blessedness as they walked to the summit together.

Yesterday you felt your heart strangely warmed. Today you have known great joy in his presence. Tomorrow will hold even more splendor than now your heart can realize. Then someday you shall see that not only the suffering in this life but the happiness too cannot be compared to the glory that shall be revealed to you when he calls you as his friend to go up higher.

IV

His friendship is everlasting.

Not long ago, I went to the hospital to see a girl whose illness is incurable. I asked the nurse if she thought it would be upsetting to the patient if I spoke to her about her relationship to Christ. I shall never forget her answer. She replied, "You don't have to ask her. I already know. When you see someone as sick as she is who has such a wonderful peace, you can know that even as the Jordan swells about her, she is being lifted by her Lord." The girl and I became friends and what the nurse said was true.

If he has walked with us in green pastures and beside still waters, our friend will not leave us when we need him most. If Jesus on the cross promised his new friend a home in Paradise, you can be assured that the grave did not dissolve their fellowship. Joined in heart at death, they are forever joined in hand in life. It is the one friendship that will never end. As dearly as you love your family, you will lose each one of them for a little while. As hard as you've worked at your business, other hands will someday occupy your tasks. I love this world that God created for us to enjoy. I am never happier than when I am in his lovely mountains that are crowned with laurels or walking beside a lovely stream as "it runs the rapid or leaps the fall." But after a bit, I shall have to bid such scenes farewell forever. But he has promised to be with me always. His friendship knows no such thing as release, no such experience as parting, no such word as goodbye.

74

The stars shine over the earth,
The stars shine over the sea,
The stars look up to the mighty God,
The stars look down on me.

The stars shall live for a million years,
A million years and a day.
But God and I will live and love
When the stars have passed away.[1]

There is a little girl in my church named Linda. She is five years old but has, I think, unusual spiritual insight. She and her little brother, Archie, were having a rather heated discussion one day. Suddenly, she turned to her daddy, who has brought her to church ever since she was a tiny baby. "Daddy," she cried vehemently, "didn't you say that Jesus rose from the grave?"

"Why yes, Linda," he said, "on Easter morning."

"There," she said to Archie triumphantly, "I told you he didn't stay dead."

And what Christ experienced, he promised to share with his friends. "He who believes in me, though he die, yet shall he live; and whoever lives and believes in me shall never die." There will be an Easter dawning for the children of the Father. But the pathway to Easter, the road to the Resurrection, can begin in our hearts today. For he said, "this is eternal life, to know God and Jesus Christ whom he has sent."

[1] From *Beyond Despair* by G. Ray Jordan. (New York, The Macmillan Co.).

CHAPTER EIGHT

Prayer

"He was praying in a certain place, and when he ceased, one of his disciples said to him, 'Lord, teach us to pray, as John taught his disciples.' "—Luke 11:1 (R.S.V.)

• Christ's followers knew that he had a power which they did not possess. They knew too the source of this strength, for many times Jesus went into the hills to pray, often before sunrise.

It is not strange then that one of his disciples requested, "Lord, tell us of your spiritual strength," or "Teach us to pray." He did not ask to be advised in the art of preaching. He did not entreat the Lord to guide him in personal counseling. He did not seek instruction from Jesus concerning the healing of disease. He felt one thing was needful—to be taught to pray. Literally, that means "teach us a prayer"; hence, Luke's account of the Lord's prayer which follows.

After presenting this beautiful pattern, Jesus tells the parable of the midnight visitor. It is the story of a man's confidence in the charity of a friend, which suggests how to pray. He closes this particular interview with positive assurance that God is not only willing, but anxious, to answer our petitions and give us the Holy Spirit.

And so we have three distinct points: what to pray, how to pray, and why we pray.

I

As Jesus shows the disciples what to pray, his very first petition is for reverence—"hallowed be thy name."

Though we are considering here that for which we pray, we must know in the first place him to whom we pray—a Father whose very name is holiness. We are turning our needy hearts to the great I Am. We are looking wistfully to the God of our fathers—Abraham, Isaac, and Jacob. We are longing for him whose name lives forever and who is remembered throughout all generations to make his divine habitation within our souls. Away with our juke-box interpretations of "The Man Upstairs," and "The Lord Is a Busy Man." A popular Hollywood actress recently referred to God as a "living doll." To hallow his name is to hold his nature in highest respect and deepest reverence. Of course God's holiness, which we wish to dwell in us, clears the haze from our horizons and we then pray for his righteousness to be not only personal but universal.

I am aware that the three words, "thy kingdom come," bear mainly eschatological or "last day" implications, but for the need in this our day, "thy kingdom come," is a

77

prayer for his love to be known, not for his territory to be seen.

Several years ago I crossed the Pacific on a small steamer with but few passengers. All of us came to know each other rather intimately. On board was an elderly Filipino named Stanley Tabao. We became good friends and often talked together. I well remember one of our last nights out from Yokohama, we were discussing the great numbers of the world's peoples who were not Christian. I commented that there were many religious people who did not even believe that the Christ had yet come. I shall never forget the earnestness and confidence with which he spoke when he said, "Stanley is but ignorant man. I not know there be people who believe Christ not come. I know this—he come for me." By his witness he explained in unforgettable words the meaning of this petition in the Lord's Prayer. The kingdom had come because the king had come.

"Give us each day our daily bread," is a petition both for temporal and spiritual necessities because we are praying for day by day strength, be it physical food or spiritual nourishment. At the same time this plea indicates not only our need but our trust. To receive the physical bread, we must as in every other endeavor co-operate with God. We sow the seed and trust him to give rain and sun to nourish and bring to fruition.

> Back of the loaf is the snowy flour,
>   And back of the flour the mill,

And back of the mill the wheat and the shower,
And the sun and the Father's will.

This is true spiritually. Jesus said, "I am the bread." Leslie Weatherhead tells about a copy of John's Gospel being picked up by a passenger on a train in India. When he discovered that it was part of the Christian scriptures, he tore it up and threw it out the window. A gang of platelayers was working on the railway line and one of them picked up a bit of paper on which was written just three words, "Bread of Life." He was so impressed that he found a Christian mission, heard the words explained, and came to know the Savior.[1] The bread will nourish but only if we eat.

The petition, "Forgive us our sins, for we ourselves forgive everyone who is indebted to us," in no way speaks of forgiveness which we are due. It tells merely of the condition we must meet. By forgiving our brethren, we are in position to seek the forgiveness of God. Elsewhere in Luke, Jesus puts it a bit plainer when he says that if you forgive you will be forgiven. There is nothing in the gospel any more important than this. In fact, it is at the very center of the Christian religion. If you have a grudge or harbor ill will toward your neighbor, your eye is not sound and your heart far from longing for God's cleansing ministry. But when peace toward your brother abides in your heart, there is no

[1] From *Over His Own Signature.*

feeling of barrier, no twinge of conscience, to keep you from desiring the redeeming presence.

The word "sin" used here means failure to be what one should be for Christ. On one occasion Peter fell down before Jesus confessing that he was a sinful man. His prayer might have been, "Forgive me. I am not what I should be. I am not what you want me to be, O Lord." Do not allow pride to keep you from praying this prayer. I know of none other we need to pray so deeply. After denying his Lord, Mark says that Peter broke down and wept. Although it is not recorded, we can safely say that not only were penitent tears shed by Simon but earnest petition was lifted for pardon. If only Judas had prayed that his sins be forgiven not only would it have saved the tragic betrayer, it would have helped the dying Savior.

"Lead us not into temptation," is a plea that God will take away the desire to sin. This petition suggests that there will be tendencies to do evil unless we wholly lean on his leading. It is a prayer not so much to resist temptation but that we will not even have the tendency in our minds to travel in its direction. To word it differently, when you walk in a store you may need to pray, "Lord, don't let me be a thief." But a far better prayer is, "Don't even allow me to think of stealing."

> Prone to wander, Lord, I feel it,
> Prone to leave the God I love;
> Here's my heart, O take and seal it,
> Seal it for Thy courts above.

Temptations come to each of us, but a heart that is sealed will be less prone to wander.

We know beyond the shadow of a doubt that God will forgive the sincere prayer of the penitent. But what influence we might wield if we would surrender our wills to Christ as the day begins instead of only confessing our sins when the evening comes! Early commitment is of more value to the kingdom than later confession. If we say with the writer of the fifth psalm, "My voice shalt thou hear in the morning, O Lord; in the morning will I direct my prayer unto thee, and will look up," we shall not have to pray with the psalmist in the sixth psalm, "O Lord, rebuke me not in thy anger, nor chasten me in thy hot displeasure."

II

The parable of the midnight visitor illustrates how to pray. It tells of a man who has suddenly become host to an unexpected guest. Having nothing for him to eat, he goes to the house of a friend on whom he knows he can depend. Since the hour is late, the friend and his family have long been in bed. He knocks on the door but finds the man reluctant to rise and supply the needed loaves. With the knuckles and perseverance of a bill collector he at last rouses his sleepy friend and his urgent request is granted.

The casual reader often misunderstands this parable. The point is not that we have to beg and plead for that which God is willing to give. We are told to ask, to seek, to knock. The Lord did not intend that we assume a continuous at-

titude of begging and pleading. The important thing to
remember about this story is that the man had a friend in
whom he had the utmost confidence. He did not believe
his friend would let him down. So in this story we see first
the man's need; then his faith; and finally his friend's response. God does always respond. Sometimes the response
is negative, but the strength his presence gives means far
more than having our desires fulfilled. The man in the
parable was given the bread by his friend. It was what he
needed. Jesus told us that we would be given what we
needed. Our supreme need however is not things but God;
not the loaves but the friend; not his gifts but his presence.

How are we to pray? We are to pray in the glad con-
sciousness that we have a friend who will not fail. He may
not grant every wish. He may not oblige each request. But
you can rest your troubled soul and anxious heart on the
tremendous truth that he knows what is best for every one
of his children and will supply every need according to his
abiding riches.

I have a friend who was a star quarterback on one of the
South's great college football teams. Many times I have
seen him kick and pass his team to victory. Just before his
senior year, he was stricken with polio. I have talked with
him about this dreadful experience and never was there
the slightest trace of bitterness in his voice. I shall never forget one afternoon when we had spoken together very intimately concerning the problem of pain and suffering rel-
ative to the will of God. As we talked of his personal atti-

tude toward these things, suddenly he spoke out with greater feeling than he had at any time during the conversation. "I could never have stood it without Christ," he said. "I can't make it now without him." We may plead and beg for things which God must refuse to give, but we have only to desire him and he will come.

III

This particular scene closes with our Lord's assuring words that by asking and seeking and knocking—that is, by desiring with all our hearts—we shall receive the Holy Spirit. This, above all others, is the reason why we pray. We do not commune with God to receive something. We enter his gates with thanksgiving and his courts with praise to receive him.

It has been said so many times, yet seldom is it believed, that you must remind yourself of this over and over again. When you go to the Lord only to get and gain, you are not really going to him at all. Petition for self plays the major role in far too many prayers. It should be minor. Not even unselfish intercession should be made central. Real prayer is unbarring the heart's door to the One who says, "Behold, I stand and knock," and bidding him enter. When you feel within your heart the joy and strength that comes with his divine presence, you will know what true prayer is.

On numerous occasions Paul requested that the Lord remove a thorn that was causing him pain. Instead of relief through comfort, Christ brought him renewal through courage, and that strength was the gift of himself.

This sacred command by Charles Wesley requires consecration we may not possess but certainly it should be our aim and prayer:

> O let us ever walk in Him,
> And nothing know beside,
> Nothing desire, nothing esteem,
> But Jesus crucified!

Years ago I read an interesting story concerning the Greek Marathon. All of the runners were preparing for the long-distance race when a young stranger walked to the starting line and presented himself as a competitor. The other men stared in awe at this tall sinewy paragon, for his long muscular legs and agile body seemed to speak of tremendous running ability. Two prizes were awarded the winner of the Marathon: a large bouquet of flowers and the privilege of standing beside the king while the remaining contests were held. Suddenly, the youthful stranger became the center of attention. One man sought to bribe him with money. Another offered property. They felt they had little chance of winning with a figure of such perfection running against them. But the young man refused these and other offers. He ran and far outdistanced his rivals. After the race had been completed and the victory won, someone asked the winning Marathoner if he thought the flowers worth more than the wealth he had refused. He answered, "I was

84

not running for the flowers. I was running so that I could stand beside my king."

That is the reason we pray. Not because of the laurels life offers or wealth the world gives, but "we lift hands of prayer for ourselves and all men so that the whole round earth may every way be bound by gold chains about the feet of God." Prayer is our gateway into the presence of the King.

CHAPTER NINE

The Bible

"Thy word is a lamp to my feet and a light to my path."
—Ps. 119:105 (R.S.V.)

• We shall never be able to pay the debt we owe for the privilege of reading the Bible. When casually we lift it from the table to read, I wonder if we ever pause and offer genuine thanks to God for this inestimable freedom. To the known patriarchs and prophets and the unknown composers who fashioned the Old Testament, we stand in eternal indebtedness and gratitude. To the evangelists and apostles who shaped for us the New Covenant, we can but bow our heads in grateful praise. God's secretaries answered their calling nobly.

But we are under great obligation not only to those who recorded the experiences that comprise the Holy Book, but to those dedicated persons who helped give us our Bible in its present-day form. We shall never know multitudes who contributed much to the Scriptures we read today, but we shall be everlastingly thankful for those who wrote diligently to give the world the Old Testament and the New Testament in their own tongues.

From the time of Jesus until the Moslem conquest, Latin was the language of the Mediterranean, and Jerome translated both Old and New Testaments into what was then the common language of the people. As time passed there was need for an English translation. The Roman Church with its clamp-like rule bitterly opposed such an endeavor by Wycliffe and later Tyndale. Both men were persecuted for their efforts and Tyndale was burned at the stake. However, the passionate desire of these two men to make God's Word and not the Roman hierarchy the authoritative voice opened the door to the Geneva Bible and the King James Version. Recently a new revision, The Revised Standard Version, has been completed and because of its clarity is inviting more and more readers to an understanding of the Word of God. There have been other translations. There have been other prominent voices. God's translators obeyed their summons admirably.

Finally, we turn with thankful hearts to those men who have appropriated and validated the message of the Scriptures in their own lives—who have found the Bible to be the great searchlight of the Spirit—and through God's grace have preached and taught its transforming message to millions. We have but to read Peter and Paul to see how even the incomplete Bible of their day inspired and influenced their ministries.

The men who have done most for the kingdom have

been those preachers who have had their own souls thrilled by the great truths of God and then have simply but passionately poured out streams of living water to the world. Clement of Rome, Origen, Chrysostom—those early spokesmen for Christ literally saturated themselves with biblical veracity. Luther and Wesley so believed the biblical stress that faith is the essential in a man knowing Christ, that they changed the entire course of the Church. Frederick W. Robertson, the father of modern homiletics, through his knowledge and use of the Bible influences more great scriptural preaching today than any man of recent times though he has been dead over a hundred years. And so Phillips Brooks and Alexander Whyte, and of late, Harry Emerson Fosdick and Leslie Weatherhead have helped transform multitudes as the Bible has spoken to and through their lives. God's expositors have done their job well.

Thus voicing the importance of the Word of God as we have, what does the Bible do for us?

I

The Bible serves as a guide for our daily walk. By this, I do not mean that we are to be told always the exact way to go. Even in our secret closets Jesus does not always reveal this to us. "Abraham went out, not knowing where he was to go." God does not always lead us along lighted ways.

We look for an answer when God speaks to Job out of the whirlwind. We read with pity of Job's great losses and suffering and the added torture imposed upon him by friends who did not understand. Perhaps we think as God speaks we shall be told the reason for it all and the solution to the problem. But we are disappointed if we are expecting a discourse from the Lord on "Some Suggestions as to Why Men Suffer" or "Handy Helps in Time of Hardship." God says absolutely nothing about grief, loss, sorrow, or pain. He tells but of his might and power and says only that he is king.

The way may not always be revealed. The trail may not always be made known. But if we read and understand his Word correctly, the Bible does more than tell of a lighted road to be walked. It fairly shouts that there is a loving hand to be held. The great truth which permeates the pages of both the Old and New Covenants is the reality not of a shining path that lies beneath us but a saving pilot who goes before us.

> Holy Spirit, faithful Guide,
> Ever near the Christian's side;
> Gently lead us by the hand,
> Pilgrims in a desert land;
> Weary souls fore'er rejoice,
> While they hear that sweetest voice,
> Whisp'ring softly, "Wanderer come!
> Follow me, I'll guide thee home."
>
> Ever present, truest Friend,
> Ever near Thine aid to lend,
> Leave us not to doubt and fear,
> Groping on in darkness drear;

When the storms are raging sore,
Hearts grow faint, and hopes give o'er,
Whisper softly, "Wand'rer come!
Follow me, I'll guide thee home."

We say the Bible is our guide because to our confused
and perplexed minds it declares that the great God of the
universe will influence and lead. Again, this does not mean
that he will always lead us out. As Lloyd Douglas reminded
us, God saves some people from storms and others in
storms. The Lord did not speak through Isaiah telling us
that we would be rescued from the raging waters. He said
something far better: "I will be with you." The author of
the ninth psalm says nothing about being taken out of his
difficult situation nor of the Lord removing the cause of dis-
tress. He says only,

The Lord is a stronghold for the oppressed,
    a stronghold in times of trouble.
And those who know thy name put their trust
    in thee,
        for thou, O Lord, hast not forsaken those who
        seek thee.

Perhaps you read of the man who was lost in the jungles
of Burma. A friendly native came to his aid and requested
the man to follow him. As the native hacked and slashed
his way through the dense thicket with his great knife, his
skeptical follower asked if he were sure this was the way.
His Burmese rescuer answered, "There is no way; I am

90

the way; follow me." [1] It is at times when there seems to be no way that we need the guidance of his word.

II

The Bible gives us strength for our particular needs. When we are discouraged and in search of one who understands and cares, we read, "I will pray the Father, and he will give you another Counselor, to be with you for ever . . . he dwells with you, and will be in you." When we are seeking to know which way to turn and help in a peculiar situation, "Commit your way to the Lord; trust in him. . . . Be still before the Lord, and wait patiently for him," can mean the difference between frustration and fruition. When we are dreading the hours before us and seemingly faced with failure, remembering that "this is the day which the Lord has made; let us rejoice and be glad in it," gives us faith to know that God did not create us for even one day of littleness or mediocrity or despair. If we cling fast to him, even disappointments become doorways to the tie that binds. When tragedy has placed her icy fingers about our throats or death has taken some loved one from us, we rest our weary hearts on this: "Even though I walk through the valley of the shadow of death, I fear no evil; for thou art with me." And when we do, the psalmist's assurance becomes our own and we strive more than ever to dwell in his house forever.

[1] Charles B. Templeton, *Life Looks Up.*

We also may turn to our Bibles and find great recipes for happiness. The advice Paul gave to the Philippians, "Rejoice in the Lord," and again, "Have no anxiety about anything, but in everything by prayer and supplication with thanksgiving let your requests be made known to God," helped them. It will serve as a remedy for worry now. When the psalmist gave as his testimony, "I will bless the Lord at all times; His praise shall continually be in my mouth," he was giving us a positive cure for despondency.

But when we speak of the Bible supplying needed strength, we are talking about far more than just assistance for melancholy moods and depressing days. It renders a greater service than simply furnishing a prescription against pessimism. It creates within our lives, if allowed, a veritable character of Christlikeness. The primary function the living word has for the written word is not to create rare moods but to establish the eternal habits of God.

The beatitudes Jesus gave to his disciples and all men are definitely good ethical views and wise conduct codes. But to say that is all is barely touching what the Master had in mind when he gave them. Being poor in spirit or humblehearted is not the philosophy a man holds; it is the life a man lives. To be hungry and thirsty for righteousness is not the occasional craving of the heart; it is the eternal appetite of the soul. To be merciful is not the view to which one caters; it is the permanent disposition of the Savior to which one is dedicated. To be pure in heart, man does not casually or incidentally lift the banner of moral excellence

92

or social tolerance; he yields his life in utter abandonment at the feet of Jesus.

The message of messages and the reality of realities that the Bible gives to our souls is this: We have God's truth for God's children forever. It constructs within our hearts that which is not passing but permanent.

An old Testament poet had nearly ceased singing and was in danger of stumbling. Then he realized the counsel of God would not fail him. Thus leaning upon new-found hope he testified, "God is the strength of my heart forever." Such Bible witness can give us courage today.

I remember one night in Hong Kong an outcast approached us and made his lustful proposition. The minister with whom I walked was used to hearing such proposals. He said nothing but held up his Bible. The vagrant had evidently had his business thwarted by such opposition before. He turned and ran swiftly away from our company. Sin always departs when we walk in the strength of the word of God.

III

The Bible reveals a Savior who will be our constant companion. That is God's first objective. That is the Bible's greatest motive. It speaks to the inward man about the personal redeemer. The Old Testament points to Jesus. The New Testament tells us about him. But that is as far as it can go. For us to be truly inspired by its message we must

93

meet face to face the Lord Jesus. That is what we mean by the Bible being validated by one's own experience.

Often we read Jesus' words to the Jews: "Search the scriptures; for in them ye think ye have eternal life: and they are they which testify of me." But we pass by those tremendously important words that follow: "Ye will not come unto me that ye might have life." I think perhaps they are the saddest words in the New Testament. The one thing that Jesus cannot do is give life when a man will not receive it. In missing Jesus the Jews missed life. They were searching for life in the scriptures. It was the wrong place. You find life in Christ and then the scriptures add to your knowledge and faith and take on new meaning as you seek to live that life. The object of the Bible is the same as was the purpose of John the Baptizer—to point men to him. If the Jews had accepted the Christ, their staid law would not have been dark and drab. Their religion would have been light and life. In fact, the law itself would have passed away for Incarnate Love had come.

And so today when men turn to the Bible not to prove points but to enrich their own lives, not to win arguments but to increase their faith, they find that its pages reveal the same life-changing Lord who will accompany and bless them as he did those on the Emmaus Road when he interpreted to them the scriptures. But he must always come first. The Scriptures meant it so. The Gospels were written because men wanted to tell of their Lord. Paul's letters

94

were written to give the struggling churches help in finding Christ.

Once, while I was serving a small church and attending school, I went to the hospital to see one who was seriously ill. It was late in the evening when I arrived and he was asleep. I left a copy of the Gospel of John with the nurse and requested that she give it to him. I had prayed for this man and though attempts had been made to interest him in the church, he never came near its doors. I returned to school that night and did not have the opportunity of visiting the hospital until the following week end. When I walked into his room, the joy on his face told me the news I had wanted to hear. "As I read the story of Jesus recorded by John," he said, "the Savior stepped from the pages into my heart." So he had, and so he will.

As the Bible becomes a lamp unto our feet and a light unto our path, the Lord Christ will use both message and messenger to lead men out of darkness to his kingdom of light.

CHAPTER TEN

Witnessing

"They went out and preached everywhere, the Lord working with them and confirming the word by the miracles that endorsed it."—Mark 16:20 (Moffatt)

• Evangelism is a word that in the twentieth century has countless times fallen among thieves. At its best it is recognized for what it is—the good news of Jesus Christ expressed through word or lived in life by any follower seeking to show another the way. At its worst it is thought of as a kind of emotional side show, consisting of one part excitement and two parts ignorance where some cantankerous barker shouts about the golden streets of heaven or the fiery flames of hell.

But real evangelism is the outreach of your personal encounter with Christ. Evangelism is not a talent developed but a life devoted. It depends not so much upon your ability as it does your consecration. You seek to live it and to witness about it because you have experienced it. A preacher friend of mine has a maid whose spiritual insights, though lovingly revealed, are often disturbing. On one occasion she reminded him, "You can't preach something you ain't got anymore than you can come back from some place you ain't been." True, but also alarming.

Andrew brought Simon Peter, his brother, to Jesus. Simon left us many great words. He must have been a thrilling evangelist. One sermon alone added three thousand souls to the kingdom. Andrew's recorded words are few, but we do have the message that won his brother, "We have met the Christ." That statement defines evangelism, for it is meeting and telling. Andrew could preach it because he had it. This is the principle upon which evangelism stands or falls—does the evangel—the good news—abide in our hearts?

Wesley could never get away from Peter Bohler's words, "Preach faith till you have it; and then, because you have it, you will preach it."

Because you have it, you will preach it. Now just as the disciples had it and witnessed to it, so may we. How did they begin?

I

First, says Mark, the disciples went out. Elsewhere it has been suggested that opportunities to present Christ will come to us. But here we are speaking about witness that takes the offensive or aggressive evangelism.

"Onward, Christian soldiers, Marching as to war." Sam Jones used to say in his own quaint manner, "There are two kinds of Christians—those that sit down and sit, and those who git up and git."

Now and then you will hear some chap say he needs to be especially impressed before he goes in quest of a man without Christ or in search of one who needs church affiliation. I certainly believe that at times the Lord will cause us to feel inclined to go in a certain direction. But some men who say they are waiting for an inclination are in reality waiting for someone else to do what they ought to be doing. Franklin Parker used to say to his students, "There's a broken heart out there somewhere and one who needs help." That is impression enough. And the Lord has promised to work with us. That is power enough. A Christian does not always wait for an opportunity to help. Sometimes he makes an opportunity to witness.

Do you remember when Saul and the other Jews were dragging the followers of Christ to prison? Such persecution led to a rather widespread scattering of those followers of the way. What did they do? It would have been easy to quit under fire, to have returned to more comfortable living and more peaceful surroundings. They also might have sat down and waited for another Pentecost, or other impressions from the Spirit, inwardly too fearful of Jewish oppression to do any marching as to war. What, I inquire again, did they do? They *went* wherever they could and preached the gospel. Philip conducted such a revival in one Samaritan town that we are told the city rejoiced. They went out. They were making opportunities.

Evangelism is as much a lay movement as it is a ministerial calling. An elderly Sunday-school teacher in England was concerned about a young chap not attending church. The boy raised guinea pigs and so the aging churchman began raising guinea pigs in an effort to gain entrance into the heart of the lad.[1] Thus he was able to go out and talk with the boy on common ground. He made his opportunity.

II

The second thing to note is the disciples preached. It seems that in many instances the supreme importance of telling the message has been neglected. But listen again to the Master's words as he prepares to preach in the cities of Galilee, "Let us go . . . that I may preach . . . for that is why I came out." When scribe and critic failed to recognize God's supreme revelation—his own son—you need not study the tactics of the disciples long until you see that preaching was their major plan for conquest. And it was the greatest apostle of them all, who in testifying to the Corinthians of his high calling said, "Christ did not send me to baptize but to preach." When we marvel at the great revival that swept England in the eighteenth century, we hear Charles Wesley sing:

> His only righteousness I show,
> His saving grace proclaim;

[1] W. E. Sangster, *Methodism Can Be Born Again.*

'Tis all my business here below,
To cry, "Behold the Lamb!"

Now since such a high premium has been placed on preaching, we must not fail whether we are ministers, mechanics, white-collar workers, housekeepers, or ditch-diggers to offer a starving world bread. The ultimate redemption of mankind depends upon minister and layman joining hands across the world to offer humanity this heavenly manna. It is not the only business of the Church but it is the main business of the Church. I like the way one layman expressed it: "I sell meat to pay expenses; my occupation is soul-winning."

I think it will do little harm to take a verse of scripture from its context in Mark's Gospel and give it a spiritual rather than physical application. Jesus had been preaching several days in the Decapolis territory. Many of the people had not had a bite to eat in three days. A few, perhaps, had brought food but this had all been eaten at least a day before. Being concerned about their welfare, Jesus said, "If I send them away hungry to their homes, they will faint on the way." Then follows the miracle of the transformation of loaves and fish and the great feast. I remember how that phrase, "If I send them away hungry," first speared its way into my soul. Since then it has become a constant challenge to my witness and charge to my preaching. As I look at the Father's children on Sundays or during the week in personal interviews, I cannot get away from those

100

haunting words, "If I send them away hungry." They are a
call to arms and cause me to promise God anew, in his
strength, the flock will be fed.

But if each of us is to witness, what is to be the content
of our message? What are the tidings we must declare?
What did the first evangelists preach?

They preached the *Cross*. They felt the Crucifixion witness would redeem all men. Do we still share that senti-
ment?

When I was in London, I visited Saint Paul's Cathedral.
On the top of the great edifice is the cross. There, like a
great beacon, it radiates its light across the vast city. I have
reached the conclusion that though there are special needs
for particular times, most sermons should not be imparted
unless there is enough of Calvary preached to bring the lost
and unconcerned unto deliverance and discipleship. It
should pour its light through all teaching. It should be the
heart beat of every message. It is vital for conversion. It is
essential for consecration. If you are not a Christian, the
Cross will speak to your longing. If you are not a witness,
the Cross will speak to your passion. If you are a disciple, it
will be your greatest hope and highest joy, for said Paul,
"Far be it from me to glory except in the cross."

I spoke of London. You read, perhaps, of the little girl
who was lost on one of its crowded streets. Some of the
kindly pedestrians sought to assist her. One asked if she
lived near Westminster, another wondered if her home
were near the House of Parliament, and question after ques-

tion was asked. Finally someone asked the child if she lived close to Charing's Cross. "Oh, yes," she answered, with smiles taking the place of tears, "take me to the Cross —I can get home from there." There is saving truth in the gospel song:

> I must needs go home by the way of the cross,
> There's no other way but this;
> I shall ne'er get sight of the gates of light
> If the way of the cross I miss.[2]

Then, they preached the Resurrection. If the Crucifixion witness would redeem all men, they felt the Resurrection witness would keep all men. One of the finest sermons Simon Peter ever preached begins,

Blessed be the God and Father of our Lord Jesus Christ, which according to his abundant mercy hath begotten us again unto a lively hope by the resurrection of Jesus Christ from the dead, to an inheritance incorruptible, and undefiled, and that fadeth not away, reserved in heaven for you, who are *kept* by the power of God.

It is by his resurrection that eternal life comes to us and we share the triumph of its truth. But again we must experience the living Christ before the witness comes.

Do you remember the two disciples who journeyed with broken spirits from Jerusalem to Emmaus? Cleopas and his companion walked with sad hearts and shattered dreams. Their hope was in the past tense. Suddenly a young stranger drew near and walked with them. Although they did not recognize him there was a mysterious something so familiar about the way he talked and a strange glory in the way he made the scriptures live, it reminded them of the One about whom they had just been speaking. I do not know how long they walked together but when they reached the home of Cleopas, they could not allow the stranger to go on. As he sat at the table with them and broke bread their eyes saw what their hearts had felt. Then Luke gives this significant word, "They knew him." Thus knowing him, what did they do? They immediately got up, their tiredness forgotten, and walked the seven miles back to Jerusalem to witness to the eleven of their risen Redeemer. The news spread. The Lord appeared again and again, and because of their living Lord, his grace and their faith gave the world a living Church. They were changed from fearful followers to dynamic disciples.

III

Finally, the disciples trusted. Mark says that the Lord worked with them. The disciples trusted, in the first place, that God would speak to them, thus giving them the message. Earlier they had been told by Jesus that when they were brought before councils and dragged before governors and kings, words would be given to them to speak. They believed that if they were given words of witness while on the defensive, they would be certain to get help from above when they took the offensive. Meanwhile, the Master's promise to send the Holy Spirit was validated and they now had the power to speak the words they were given.

In saying this, I do not mean to imply that God dictates all sermons to ministers. Now, I think more suggestions for sermons would come if we read our Bibles in order to gain spiritual nourishment instead of primarily seeking a text. At least I have found this to be true as I have read devotionally.

And I am certainly not suggesting that anyone lay aside his books, paper and pen, walk confidently into the pulpit unprepared and say, "All right, Lord, fill me up." But I am saying that when we commit our all to him, when we do our best in preparation and prayer, we can expect God to do something in our lives and with our testimonies.

Sometimes I have found in my own ministry that even after careful preparation, the Lord channeled my thoughts along a different line. This I believe to be inspiration, but the Lord can better inspire the man who has prepared.

The greatest inspiration the Lord gives is through prayer. This is true in every field ripe for witnessing. No matter how practiced you are in personal evangelism, no matter the many avenues of approach with which you may be familiar, nothing substitutes for the inward voice: "Thus saith the Lord."

I am thinking of a layman with whom I have visited a great deal. It would be amazing to count the number of

104

men he has introduced to Christ. But the more powerful he became in his witnessing, the more faithful he became in his praying. The fact that he was a fruitful evangel was because he grew increasingly willing to rely fully on Jesus.

Paul felt that he had failed in his ministry to the people of Athens. Hence, when he arrived at Corinth, he announced that he would be constantly preaching two sermons: Jesus Christ and Jesus Christ the crucified. How did he come to this decision? Not through reading up on the matter nor from spiritual advice received from his preacher brethren. He had been more closely associating with his companion of the Damascus road, and by trusting him, had been given the two subjects of supreme importance.

The disciples trusted, in the second place, that God would speak through them, thus reaping the harvest. Mark tells us that the Lord confirmed the word. That word confirm means to establish. God will take care of the results. It took me a long time to see this, actually many disturbing days and restless nights. But God did not call me to be a successful witness; he called me to be a faithful witness. He did not tell me to achieve but believe. He did not tell me to accomplish but to trust. The Lord says that his word will not return to him empty. If we will speak it, he will bless it. Wherever you may be working, whatever you may be doing, there is a vineyard of service. You do not have to be concerned about being used, only about being usable. If you speak for Christ with your lips and life, God will confirm and glorify. He that bears seed for sowing, "shall come home with shouts of joy bringing his sheaves with him."

Once I was invited to conduct a revival in a church that was notorious for its coldness. I was familiar with the situation for I had often attended services there. Many of the members were indifferent and the morality of the town where the church was located was considered rather low. I therefore came near to refusing acceptance. During the time immediately prior to the meeting I wished I had. The outlook to me seemed dark and I became very discouraged. Finally, as I grew more and more tense, I did what I should have when I first received the invitation. Remembering the assuring words that God would work through his children to do his pleasure, I turned the services, the church, the people in need, and all else over to him. I confessed to the Master that if anything were done, he would have to do it. I promised to do the best I could but I would allow his Spirit to take charge from there. Now explain it how you will, the Holy Spirit moved upon that church with great power. The entire atmosphere of the church was changed. Many of those who yielded to Christ's call are now leaders in the spiritual activity of that town and many came into a real and radiant relationship with God they had never known before.

Of course preparation and prayer by some of the faithful members helped mightily to pave the way, but for my own part, God could not have used me until I put everything in his hands.

Trust God to speak to your life and through your witness. Not all whom you seek for the Savior will be found. But victorious faith will help you point many who are lost to the Father and home.

CHAPTER ELEVEN

The Church

"I commend unto you Phebe our sister, which is a servant of the church which is at Cenchrea."—Rom. 16:1

• Paul wrote a letter to the church at Rome and Phebe carried it. In this letter to the Romans Paul refers both to Phebe and to himself as servants. Frank Boreham has suggested that regardless of one's eminence, to be a servant is to hold a position of supreme importance. Any service that is done for Jesus is big business. On Sunday morning I pray for the ushers, the ones who receive the offering, those that greet the people as they reach the church doors, and others who perform similar duties, just as I pray for those who preach and teach and sing. A friendly welcome, a warm smile, and a firm handshake sometimes ring the bell in a man's heart where the sermon, anthem, and lesson fail.

When a man accepts Christ as his Savior and joins his Church, he takes the gallant pledge of servanthood. All Christendom is held together by the sons and daughters of the king whose hearts and hands have become devoted servants. Here are four things a good servant can do.

I

A good servant attends Church.

There are two reasons why you should go to church. In the first place, you need the church. Paul exhorted the church at Ephesus to grow up in every way into Christ. I cannot and do not see how any man can be growing in the grace of God and not have a vital relationship with his church. I need the fresh inspiration and renewing of hope which my church supplies. I covet for my own experience contact with those of like spirit and similar passion who make my dedication all the more precious.

In connection with this, I can best speak from my own life. I gave my life to Christ just before I became nineteen. My youth had been rather stormy and stained. I desired to leave home and attend college and work where I was not known. This is by no means essential. In some cases after conversion it is best for one to stick his ground come what may. In my own situation I think venturing to new surroundings was preferable. The church gave me my first opportunity to preach. Twice a month I would journey a few miles from the college community to speak in a small country church. How those kind, Godly folk of the hills ever put up with me, I don't know. Yet, I think that even when one stumbles and often falls and fails, the people will know he is doing his sincere and honest best. The more mistakes

I made, the more petitions they lifted for me. After being gone for years, I went back to see some of the faithful just to thank them for loving me and believing in me and holding my high calling constantly in the Master's hand. It was the Church that opened its door to my youthful eagerness and nurtured my first childish steps up the mountain. It is still the Church that tells me regardless of my inadequacies and stumblings, I can yet put on the whole armor of Christ.

You were in the hospital weakened by illness and thoroughly depressed. It was the Church with its blessed ministry of encouragement through prayer, in the form of both pastor and laymen, who kept vigil by your bed.

You were tempted to compromise and yet were not willing to yield to your soul's decay. You sought the Church, and its steeple pointing to the sky seemed to say that you too had an eternal direction from which you must not turn. The world had trampled on your feet and cynicism sought access into the citadel of your soul. It was then that the voice of the Church proclaimed, "Ask, and you will receive, that your joy may be full." The voice stirred you into desiring what God wished to give and you arose in newness of life. The church will not fail now, for

> From vict'ry unto vict'ry
> His army shall He lead,
> Till every foe is vanquished,
> And Christ is Lord indeed.

In the second place, the Church needs you. There is someone that only your influence may reach and only your inspiration can lift. I am not speaking of those who are excellent prayers, or players, or speakers, or singers. I am talking not about the talented sacrifices but the living sacrifices.

I was driving my car in a certain city not long ago attempting to find a particular street. I pulled up beside a man and asked if he could help me. The man, though dumb, was not deaf. He could not speak but he pointed in the direction which I was to go. What a marvelous asset it would be for the kingdom if we talked less and pointed more—to Christ!

"We have churches," wrote P. T. Forsyth, "of the nicest, kindest people who have nothing apostolic or missionary, who never knew the soul's despair or its breathless gratitude." Next to one's own awareness of sin and salvation, the greatest despair and most glorious gratitude comes as we seek the unchurched and point them to the valiant servanthood against which the gates of Hell shall not prevail.

II

A good servant prays.

Already prayer has been discussed. But we are concerned at this particular point about praying for our Church. Sometimes you may be unable to attend the worship service. Financially, you may be able to give but little. Many lack the talent and ability they should like to possess. However, there is one rewarding experience you can share with the saints. You can pray for the Church and its ministry to the world.

Now when you pray for the Church what does it accomplish? First, it gives power to its ministers. One Sunday morning Spurgeon was asked by a visitor to England the secret of his preaching power. The great minister led the tourist away from the sanctuary and multitude. He took him to a room where men and women were on their knees lifting their preacher to heaven. "This," said Spurgeon, "is why I can speak for my Lord."

Paul knew this. How earnestly he solicited the prayers of not only the saints but of the struggling young churches. He asked the church at Ephesus to pray for him that he might speak boldly the mystery of the gospel and declare it as he ought. There are pulpits across the world today which lack energy and strength because the churches have not prayed for the men who preach in them.

Peter was in prison but Luke tells us that earnest prayer for him was made to God by the Church. And the chains fell off! I think how many times I have been bound by the fetters of inadequacy and inability. But some of God's people, loyal in prayer, lifted me in loving intercession. That is the only way I can explain the strange and glorious consequences resulting.

Praying for the Church gives unity to its purpose. Of course the pre-eminent program of the Church is to redeem the world. It should be the main petition in the prayer life

112

of our people. Jesus said that if the eye is single, the whole body shall be full of light. If prayer within the will of God were unselfishly and devotedly made, it is impossible to say how far the Church's light would shine. Those attempting to build the church in Jerusalem had their most refreshing hour on the day of Pentecost; but to see why, we have to remember the days and nights of prayer which preceded. Luke speaks of the men and women who with one accord devoted themselves to prayer.

Prayer gives dedication to the church membership. When Jesus prayed for the disciples then and his disciples now, he prayed that we all might be one in his and the Father's love. It is this way above all others that we are drawn to the heart of God. There are many paths to high spiritual attainment. But prayer is the soul's grandest highway to God's fullness.

One of the great hymns of Christendom is "The Church's One Foundation." The last verse begins: "Yet she on earth hath union with God the Three in One." That dedicated union is made possible by the prayers of true believers.

III

A good servant gives.

Much of the kingdom's work must be financed. Our gifts assist in furthering the gospel claims. I have known some men who, if they supported their homes the way they contribute to the Church, would not have a decent meal on the table or an electric light burning in the house. Our

113

Church must build hospitals, send missionaries, train ministers, construct churches. It must uphold every cause that is spiritual, be it care for the homeless or sending the good news out by radio and television. The Church needs your contribution, your money, so that its message may go further and its opportunity be greater. But the youngest child in his Sunday school can tell you this. Our earnest wish at this point is that men know the great joy that can be theirs through giving. There is a strong relationship between a man giving his life and his pocketbook to Christ. Paul felt this way. He said the churches of Macedonia gave beyond their means; but he added, "First they gave themselves to the Lord." I pray this point will be impressed upon us.

Sometimes in various services I have attended, both minister and layman appeared apologetic when the time for the offering drew nigh. I am not sure that praying or reading the Word of God are more sacred expressions of worship than giving of our possessions to the Master. Hearing the written word and listening for the living word are both receptions. But by sharing our means, we become doers of the Word and not hearers only. And it was Jesus himself who said, "It is more blessed to give than to receive.

This is not a sermon on tithing, although I recommend it to bring new splendor into the treasury of your dedication. Up and down the land, wherever I meet good servants of the cross, these men and women are forever telling me that their supreme joy is giving. Most of us would not be hurt materially by giving a tenth, even so God compensates in the heart for what one misses in the purse.

Remember that the sum of the gift is not as important as the soul of the giver. Not long ago on the concluding night of a week of special services, the church took a love offering for those directing the endeavor. After the benediction had been pronounced and I had spoken briefly with some of the people, I walked out the door and down the street beside the church. Suddenly I heard little feet running after me. I turned just as she got to me all out of breath. Hurriedly, but oh! how emphatically, she said as she placed a small coin in my hand, "This is all I have. I didn't have anything to give the song leader but I thought you could use this for Jesus." It was just a quarter's worth of silver, but it was a million dollar's worth of love. The thing vital in giving is not the amount of it but the dedication of it. "The gift without the giver *is* bare."

IV

A good servant renders service.

I have always thought that this word service had more to do with loyalty than talent. Will you be loyal to the Church? Will you be faithful to the cause of Christ? We are success-minded in our Twentieth Century as at no other time in history. There are few people who have not been bitten by the "get it done" bug; indeed, chewed to pieces. But getting it done and being successful does not always insure one's spiritual progress. In the realm of the

115

material, a businessman can be successful and show no fidelity to the Church whatsoever. A college graduate may have gotten it done when he finished with scholastic honors, but yet be far from the Lord. On the other hand, you may never be the good servant you desire to be. Browning said the reach should exceed the grasp. You may never lead multitudes to the gates of new life. Man sees what we attain, but God knows what we attempt. That which matters most is faithfulness in your efforts to serve. You may not accomplish the greatest but you can certainly be true to the Highest.

I have always felt great pity in my heart for Jeremiah. Although I consider him the greatest of the prophets, he was the most disliked man in Judah. He had no wife nor family in whom he could confide. He had no backers to support him. Kings respected but hated him, and the priests would gladly have killed him if they could. So far as we know he never won a convert and never saved a soul. But it was his reliance upon God and his close personal awareness of him and relationship to him that reminds one of Jesus Christ more than any man in the Old Testament. He was jeered by the multitude and constantly persecuted, yet the burning fire in his heart could not be put out. Successful? Is a cistern a fit home for the victor or being stoned proper pay-off for the winner? Yet through over forty years of hardships in the midst of a faithless people who walked the valleys, we remember him as the mountain-man of faith.

I am thinking of a man whose legs were cut off halfway

116

between his knees and hips. He made a small wagon and Sunday after Sunday pushed himself up the hill to his church. I doubt if he could sing a solo. I don't suppose he could have offered a public prayer. But by going to church, his was the most powerful witness given in that town for Jesus Christ. He was a good servant. God help us to be!

CHAPTER TWELVE

The Mind of Christ

"Let this mind be in you, which was also in Christ Jesus."
—Phil. 2:5

• Possessing the mind of Christ is the aim of every fervent follower. It is the dedicated desire of each true disciple. Everything said heretofore has pointed to this. I am glad Paul used the word "mind." It speaks of permanence and completeness. To have the mind of Christ is not to occasionally entertain an idea that is charitable. It is to have the permanent disposition of the Master. It is complete, for if a man has the mind of Christ it is because the mind of Christ has the man.

In his very excellent translation of the Epistles, J. B. Phillips expresses this thought in these words: "Let Christ Himself be your example as to what your attitude should be."

We need the mind of Christ in every phase of life. Four areas are to be mentioned where his abiding attitude is essential if we are to receive God's fullness.

I

We need the mind of Christ in our thinking. Never has one spoken more wisely or correctly than the Old Testament writer who said, "As a man thinketh in his heart, so is he." We become like our thoughts; in reality, our thoughts make us. Disraeli said, "Nurture your mind with great thoughts; to believe in the heroic makes heroes."

Paul wrote the Philippian church, "Whatsoever things are true, whatsoever things are honest, whatsoever things are just, whatsoever things are pure, whatsoever things are lovely, whatsoever things are of good report . . . think on these things." Paul knew that if a man is thinking truth, he will come to be true. If a man is thinking honesty, he tends to become honest. If a man is thinking justice, he will seek to be just. If a man is thinking purity, he will be pure. If a man has his mind fixed on love, his life will become lovely. If a man is thinking on things of good report, he will become gracious in his actions and character. All of these admirable attitudes are ours because God has taken possession of our minds.

Then, if Christ can get a man dedicated in mind, He can get a life consecrated to usefulness. Jesus knew that herein lay Simon's difficulty. When Peter promised to be faithful he was never more sincere. But he was fickle and flighty not because he was wicked but because he did not possess the permanent disposition of his Lord. When the Master met him on the seashore and told him to feed his

sheep, he was not suggesting a week of preaching. He was
pleading for a lifetime of service. Peter finally became the
shepherd the Savior wanted him to be because little by little
in communion's quiet moments, he had come to have the
mind of Christ.

> Each nobler service that men have wrought
> Was first conceived as a fruitful thought;
> Each worthy cause with a future glorious
> By quietly growing becomes victorious.

II

We need the mind of Christ in our speaking. The words
we say give testimony as to whether or not we are his disciples. Jesus said that our words would justify us or con-
demn us. The writer of Ecclesiastes advised us not to
allow our mouths to lead us into sin. If our tongues can
lead us into sin, they cause us then to suffer sin's penalty.
Now, just how important is it that we have consecrated lips?
What words are sinful?

First, lying words are sinful. Of course there are two ways
we lie. We lie by the things we say and we lie by the things
we don't say. Potiphar's wife attempted to make Joseph
share in sinful conduct. He refused but the officer's wife,
enraged for being rejected, informed her husband that
Joseph had tried to force her to commit adultery. This lie
cost Joseph his position and his freedom.

If there is any difference, the worst of the two is failure
to use the right word or to not speak at all. Lincoln said,

120

"To sin by silence when they should protest makes cowards out of men." We know that when the crowd came to take Jesus prisoner the disciples all forsook him and fled. They were afraid. They had promised to be faithful but they offered not even a word at his trial or execution. They lied not with their lips but with their lives.

Next, profane words are sinful. All of us know it is wrong to use profanity. A commandment with which we have always been familiar is, "You shall not take the name of the Lord your God in vain." But how many of us are guilty, as day after day in our private conversations we fail to speak the language of our Lord. We are profane if we find shady stories to our liking. It is especially needful that those who call themselves by his name have clean hearts and dedicated lips. Some years ago I heard a preacher friend say something that I have never forgotten. "We ministers may tell our laymen jokes which are unbecoming to God's ambassadors," he said. "Someday when we preach on 'Blessed are the pure in heart, for they shall see God,' they will think that is a joke, too."

Then, careless or gossiping words are sinful. These are the words we speak off the record; they are the words that need not be spoken. The world would get on a great deal better without them. Hearts might not be broken if they went unsaid. How great would be our influence for the kingdom should we hear idle gossip and let it go no further. Should you meet a person thoroughly convinced that the choice bit of scandal he is telling is true, and say

121

nothing, it would perhaps irritate him but it might also cause him to do less talking and more considering. James Whitcomb Riley might have had this in mind when he wrote:

> Let the other fellow wrangle
> Till the storm has blown away,
> Then he'll do a heap o' thinking
> 'Bout the things you didn't say.

After the fire and earthquake that almost destroyed San Francisco in 1906, giant billboards were erected throughout the city reading: "Don't talk earthquake; talk business." Do not forget that the most important subject about which you can converse is the business of Jesus.

III

We need the mind of Christ in our loving. We have already spoken about God's searching love for man and of love being the greatest indication of conversion. Here we should like to dwell upon Christ's great statement, "by this shall all men know that you are my disciples, if you have love one to another." Two points need stressing.

First, it will not be easy to love everyone. There are some people that it is just as natural to love as it is to receive the sunlight. I have known some fragrant souls whom to meet was like walking into a rose garden. Such a spirit, I am certain, possessed Barnabas. His name means "Son of

122

encouragement." When Paul needed help, he found strength in Barnabas. When John Mark had shown his cowardice, it was Barnabas who stood by him. You can no more help loving a man like that than you can help breathing. But there are some for whom it is difficult to have affection. That is why it is imperative for God's love to entirely possess you. Indeed, it may be impossible to love certain people without the touch of his hand on our hearts.

Do you remember when Paul stood before the council at Jerusalem and the high priest ordered that he be slapped? Paul did not respond by suggesting a few quiet moments of meditation. He did not even recite a bit of his famous sermon on charity. He said, "God shall strike you, you white washed wall!" I am persuaded that the apostle had to do considerable praying before he came to love Ananias.

Here is the more important aspect. It is our love for people that proves we are his children. We have been commanded by our Savior to search and find other disciples. We have been instructed to baptize and teach them. Now this is possible only when we have allowed Christ entrance into our lives. In other words, when we go out, it is an indication that he has come in.

I shall not forget when the saintly Kagawa told me his favorite verse of scripture. It was, "He that loveth not knoweth not God; for God is love." I can yet see the little tubercular who weighed less than a hundred pounds standing in church with the light of the Lord on his face. I can still remember how he said, "If I had it to do over, my life

would be used just as it has been." And when I think of
Kagawa's influence on not only Japan but all the world, I
pray with greater earnestness than ever before, "O God,
help me to know thee, and in knowing thee to love thy
children everywhere, for thou art love."

This love must go out to the alcoholic and those who
are bound by similar chains and tell them there is One who
can set them free. This love must prod and push into the
slum sections where lights are low and souls are lower and
share its blessed tidings of redemptive mercy. This love
must inform the prejudiced mind that God's gospel is not
for the white man only. And at the same time such love
must speak to the world's varying colors, saying, "Whoso-
ever will may come." This love must cross oceans, climb
mountains, erect churches, build schools, and plant crops.
For love is the missionary zeal that goes to "the dark places
of earth's needy races," and testifies that the kingdom has
come indeed.

IV

We need the mind of Christ in our dedication. I know
of few testimony songs more true than this one:

> But we never can prove
> The delights of His love,
> Until all on the altar we lay;
> For the favor He shows,
> And the joy He bestows,
> Are for them who will trust and obey.

That is why we remember the poor widow's gift; not because it was much, but because it was all. If Heaven is not at your fingertips and if that joy that thrills is absent from your life and witness, it may be because Christ cannot say of you as he said of her, "She has given all her living."

Now this happy privilege is possible for each one of us now. It is available because he is available. The Master knew that Calvary meant the giving of his life. So he prayed the night he was seized, "For their sake I consecrate myself." That prayer was for his disciples then but it was also for you and me. It was by his commitment that they were committed. It is by his dedication that we are dedicated. By the giving of himself, we have the daily opportunity to give ourselves.

While traveling in France, I went to see the great palace at Versailles. Built during the reign of Louis XIV, it is a masterpiece of architecture. There are hundreds of rooms and I was told that over a thousand people could be accommodated. Some of these rooms have names. There is the Room or Hall of Mirrors where the world's leaders met after the first Great War. There is the Room of Music, and the Room of Chandeliers, and many others. I remember one room especially. The guide said it was known as the Room of Abundance. Here men came weary with travel, hungry and thirsty after a day's journey on the dusty road. They were fed and refreshed and royally entertained.

God has a room of abundance. It is open to the world's

weary and the seeking. It has been prepared for the world's hungry and thirsty. To enter with your whole heart is to have the mind of Christ; it is to receive God's fullness. In this room we shall feel at home, for in it is fullness of joy and at his right hand there are pleasures forevermore.